THE JOY I SEEK

FRAGMENTS FROM "ENDYMION: A POETIC ROMANCE"
BY JOHN KEATS

THE JOY I SEEK

Preface by Louis Martz
Introduction & Paintings by David Finn

FRAGMENTS FROM "ENDYMION: A POETIC ROMANCE"
BY JOHN KEATS

MADISON BOOKS

For Laura

Published by Madison Books
4720 Boston Way
Lanham, Maryland 20706

12 Hid's Copse Road
Cumnor Hill, Oxford OX2 9JJ, England

Distributed by National Book Network.

Designed and Produced by Ruder·Finn Design

ISBN: 1-56833-240-8

Printed and bound in the United States by Public Relations Production Co., Inc and Bridge Port Bindery

Excerpts from Endymion: A Poetic Romance from
John Keats, A Critical Edition of the Major Works.
The Oxford Authors, Oxford University Press, 1990.

Contents

Preface

BY LOUIS L. MARTZ

In a letter of 1817, as John Keats was beginning to write *Endymion: A Poetic Romance,* he defended the writing of a long poem by saying:

> *Do not the Lovers of Poetry like to have a little Region to wander in where they may pick and choose, and in which the images are so numerous that many are forgotten and found new in a second Reading: which may be food for a Week's stroll in the Summer?*

David Finn has read the poem in this way, picking and choosing passages that suit his theme of love, with the result, as he says in his introduction, that he has "created a new poem, both visual and verbal, where each passage, in this new arrangement, leads on to the next." The unity of this new sequence is sustained visually by the constant coloration of blues and greens, sometimes intermingled, sometimes appearing separately, until, in Image 44, they blend with other colors to lead us out into some transcendent region. It is a kind of "stroll in the Summer," where the varied blues and greens of nature, in earth, sea, and sky work together to express a central theme of Keats's poem: that humankind is part of nature, responding to the forces that underlie the greenness of grass and the blueness of waters and sky.

All this is expressed in the painting (Image 2) that arises from the poem's most famous line: "A thing of beauty is a joy for ever." Here we see the human figure surrounded by, or immersed in, or emerging from the medley of blues and greens, a technique repeated in many of the images of passion that follow. But frequently, when we might expect some explicit scene of sexual passion to appear in the painting, we meet instead an abstraction. This is quite in line with the Keatsian theme that links the physical and the spiritual, to show how Endymion's quest is answered at the close of the poem in the fusion of the Indian Maid with the moon goddess. Thus Image 10, arising from a passage of explicit sensuousness, presents a curving figure worthy of Hans Arp, the white form held within the tones of green and blue. Image 13, arising from an especially sensuous set of verses, presents the human form moving toward a state of abstraction. Similarly, the "naked waist" of Image 18 is an almost pure abstraction of the human form. David Finn is following out the view expressed by Kandinsky and Mondrian, that the spiritual in art is best expressed, perhaps can only be expressed, by abstraction.

Consequently, in the latter part of the sequence, as the paintings of human passion become more and more explicitly erotic, the number of abstract paintings increases to match the realistic representation of physical love. And at the same time, the dominant blues and greens appear in redoubled strength, as though to indicate the unity of sense and spirit, as in Keats, through images of nature. Thus, the sequence presents the "regular stepping of the Imagination towards a truth" that Keats describes in a letter of 1817 related to the line "Wherein lies happiness?"

Sometimes a sly humor seems to show through the ecstatic imagery of Finn's paintings. The "hovering feet, / More bluely vein'd, more soft, more whitely sweet / Than those of sea-born

Venus" seem in Image 19 to be the sturdy realistic feet of a woman who is relaxing her weary feet in the waters. And the dancing figures of the maidens in Image 7 or the figures "sailing" through "the dizzy sky" in Image 34 refuse to be taken solemnly. The "joy" that inspires the whole sequence is filled with happy surprises, as sense and spirit blend in a panorama of realistic passion and spiritual abstraction.

In all these ways, David Finn has carried out the inspiration he has found in the opening lines of "Endymion," not only in the lines quoted as preface to the poem, but also in the lines that follow, where Keats finds solace from the woes of society in images of nature:

Therefore, on every morrow, are we wreathing
A flowery band to bind us to the earth,
Spite of despondence, of the inhuman dearth
Of noble natures, of the gloomy days,
Of all the unhealthy and o'er-darkened ways
Made for our searching: yes, in spite of all,
Some shape of beauty moves away the pall
From our dark spirits.

Such is the effect of the many shapes of beauty that David Finn presents, human figures and subtle abstractions living within the "green world" of Keats's poem.

Introduction

BY DAVID FINN

Endymion: A Poetic Romance is the long poem Keats wrote at the age of 21 in what he described as a feverish attempt to write 4,000 lines in something like nine months. Despite its unevenness, there "blows through it," as Matthew Arnold put it, "the breath of genius." Its greatest passages achieve heights of expression that may be unsurpassed in the English language.

For me, the glorious lines Keats wrote have been an inspiration of a lifetime. When I was 21, I was serving in the armed forces during World War II, and one of a handful of books that I carried with me wherever I went was a volume of Keats' collected poems. I used to read his lines in moments of relaxation, and the magic of his phrases filled my mind with awe about a world of love and beauty. I was as innocent as he was at the time, and his words gave wings to my dreams as they must have given to his.

The story of Endymion never held any great interest for me. I knew virtually nothing of Ovid and his accounts of Venus, Adonis, Pan, Diana, Apollo, and the rest. The characters in the poem—Endymion, Peona, Cynthia, Glaucus, the Indian maid—meant as little to me as the elements of the plot. There were many episodes in the poem that baffled me, and I wondered what the point was of sending Endymion on so many different adventures. Yet what caught my eye and aroused my senses were the exquisite phrases I came across here and there in the long poem, about a heaven of gentle limbs, blush-tinted cheeks, kissing breasts, shining hair, wooing arms, hovering feet, honey words—all of which inspired the passionate dreams and longings of two 21-year-olds, Keats and me!

When I was much older, I returned to "Endymion" with an entirely new perspective. By then other poems had made their mark on my consciousness and I had a very different point of view toward life and love and heaven.

When I was in my late forties and fifties, I had become obsessed with T.S. Eliot's *Four Quartets* (which he wrote when he was about the same age), and I was overwhelmed by its revelations of spiritual truths, barely visible in the dark, impenetrable mystery of human existence. I had been a painter all my life and I decided at that time to produce a series of paintings that expressed on canvas my reactions to the lines of that great poem. Later, it was Yeats's two "Byzantium" poems that touched my heart most deeply, and I produced another series of paintings that attempted to show my appreciation for the poet's celebration of art and music and poetry as the means of transcending the befuddling enigma of life and death.

Then when I was in my sixties, "Endymion" came back into my life, this time not as the fantasy of a youth dreaming of embraces I had never known, but as the brilliant description of the joys I had experienced as an adult. What Keats and I had imagined as youthful innocents, I had known as a happily married man whose passion had grown ever stronger through the years. I now found in the lines of "Endymion" a perfect description of the great love that had been the blessing of my life.

And so my next creative venture was a series of paintings to capture the new meaning Keats's words had for me. It was not the long poem with its many episodes that I wanted to depict, but rather the rapture of two souls joining as one, physically and spiritually, that had been at the heart of my personal life. His magnificent lines struck me as one of the most beautiful descriptions of the love between a man and a woman I had ever read—equaling if not surpassing Solomon's *Song of Songs.* And since they told the story of my greatest intimacies, my canvases were like a series of self-images, not of myself physically, but of what I saw and felt in my life of love.

It seemed strange to me, as a man in my sixties, to find such a strong identification with the words of a young man who had died at the age of 25. Keats probably had little more experience of love than an intensely passionate but short-lived romance with his next-door neighbor, Fanny Brawne. Although they did become engaged, he fell ill with tuberculosis and died before they could be married. But the imagination of a great poet can see beyond his own immediate experience and compose phrases that are timeless. That my life has been as glorious as his dreams made the impact of his words all the more powerful.

There is no doubt that this poem, Keats's first major work, was a towering achievement. And the word "towering" is particularly apt, for it is not the entire landscape of the poem that is so inspired, but the peaks of expression that appear every now and then above the hills and valleys of the story. From my point of view, the poem would have touched my heart at any age if it had been a fraction of its length. I felt that if the heights that he had reached could have been joined together, it would have been the Mt. Everest of poetic expression, free of the uncertain wanderings of an overanxious storyteller.

In my series of paintings I decided to ignore the story of "Endymion" and to focus on the passages that I thought were Keats at his best. As I invented images to accompany those lines, I experienced the joys of his marvelous phrases without worrying about what was happening to his characters. I could paint images that were inspired by my life's experiences rather than try to follow the tale he was telling.

When I finished the series of 44 paintings, I photographed them, and to see how they would fit together, I mounted small Polaroid prints in a little book that I made up, copying the relevant passages on the opposite pages. It was pleasing to have them all together, but when I turned the pages, I was somewhat dismayed to find that the result was disjointed. Past and present tenses were mixed at random, the object of the romance was sometimes addressed as "thee" and sometimes referred to as "she." The subjects didn't follow one another in any sensible manner. All the words and paintings were from the same poem and were in the same mood, but the collection didn't hold together. And although my original purpose of creating images that could stand on their own as individual paintings was achieved, when I put them together in a sequence based on their position in the poem, the effect was chaotic.

I therefore tried another, completely unorthodox, approach to ordering the sequence of the paintings. My new idea was to see if the paintings and words could be made to follow each other in a way that made sense from an entirely different point of view. The story didn't matter; in fact there was no story that could be read from the paintings and passages I had selected. I just wanted to find a way to show what these words and images meant to me. And after shuffling the photographs and words back and forth I finally came up with an order I thought worked. I knew that in effect I was creating a new poem, but I thought Keats might forgive me since I had merely strung his words together in a new way. And to be true to the poem in its original form, I indicated on each page the lines and section of the poem from which the words were taken.

A great love poem emerged as a result, one that I had imagined in my mind's eye but had never before been able to see as a discrete entity. Read in this way, "Endymion" is not a story of adventure, of a god seeking the mythical object of his love through a long and circuitous route. It is a song of love that soars into the heavens as two lovers embrace and feel the joy of their flesh joined together in a supreme and immortal embrace.

The paintings are for the most part based on images that are very personal to me—whether a portrait of my beloved, or the glories of her ageless beauty, or pastoral scenes recalling happy memories. In some instances I have created abstract forms to express the sentiment of the passage, but most of the paintings are purposely descriptive. In that sense, the paintings tell the story of my life. Accompanied by the words of "Endymion" in their new order, they reveal a lifelong passion that has been the heart of my being.

THE JOY I SEEK

FRAGMENTS FROM "ENDYMION: A POETIC ROMANCE"
BY JOHN KEATS

1

Wherein lies happiness? In that which becks
Our ready minds to fellowship divine,
A fellowship with essence, full of shine
Full alchemized, and free of space. Behold
The clear religion of heaven!

Book I 777-781

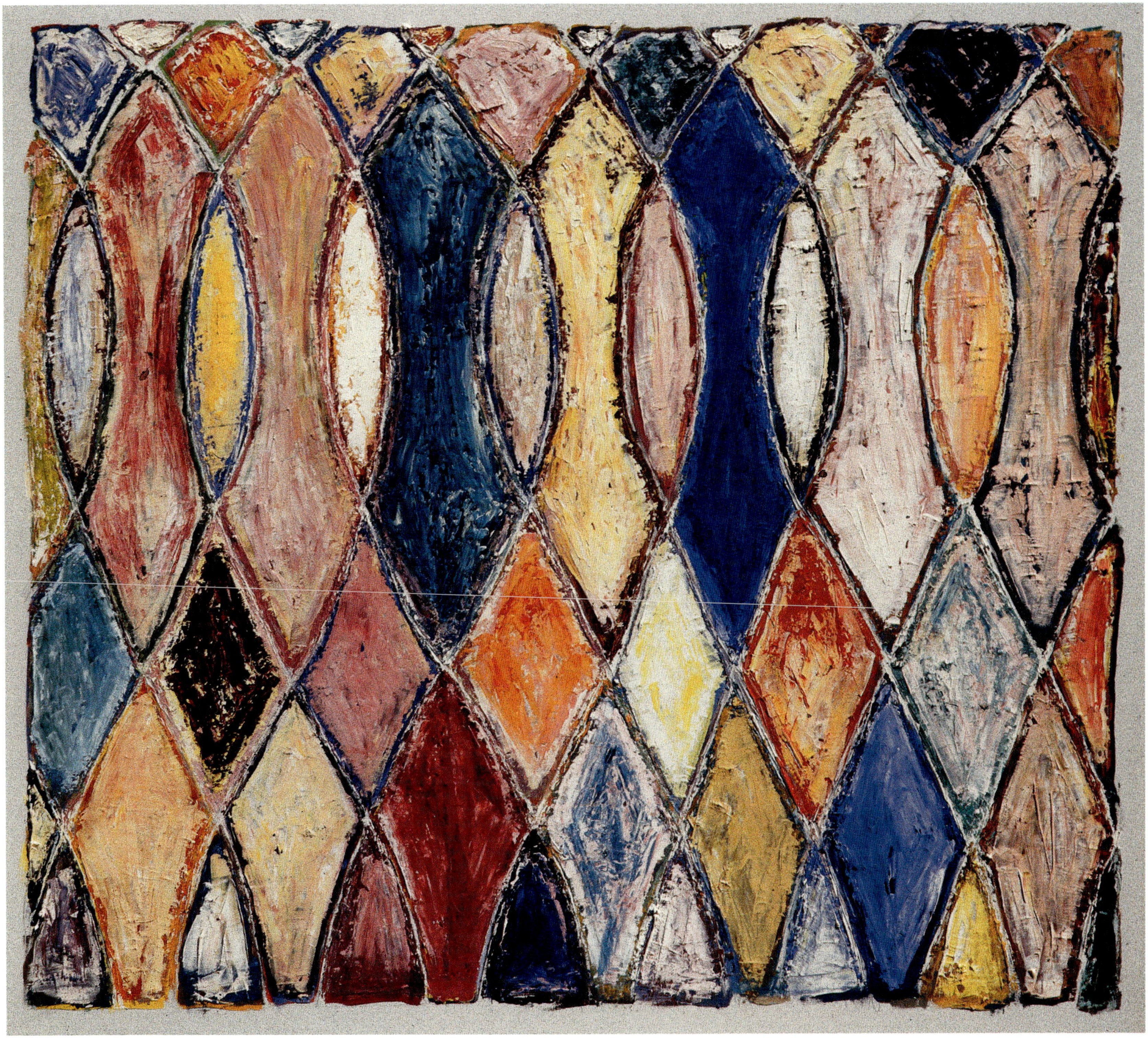

2

A thing of beauty is a joy for ever:
Its loveliness increases; it will never
Pass into nothingness; but still will keep
A bower quiet for us, and a sleep
Full of sweet dreams, and health, and quiet breathing.

Book I 1-5

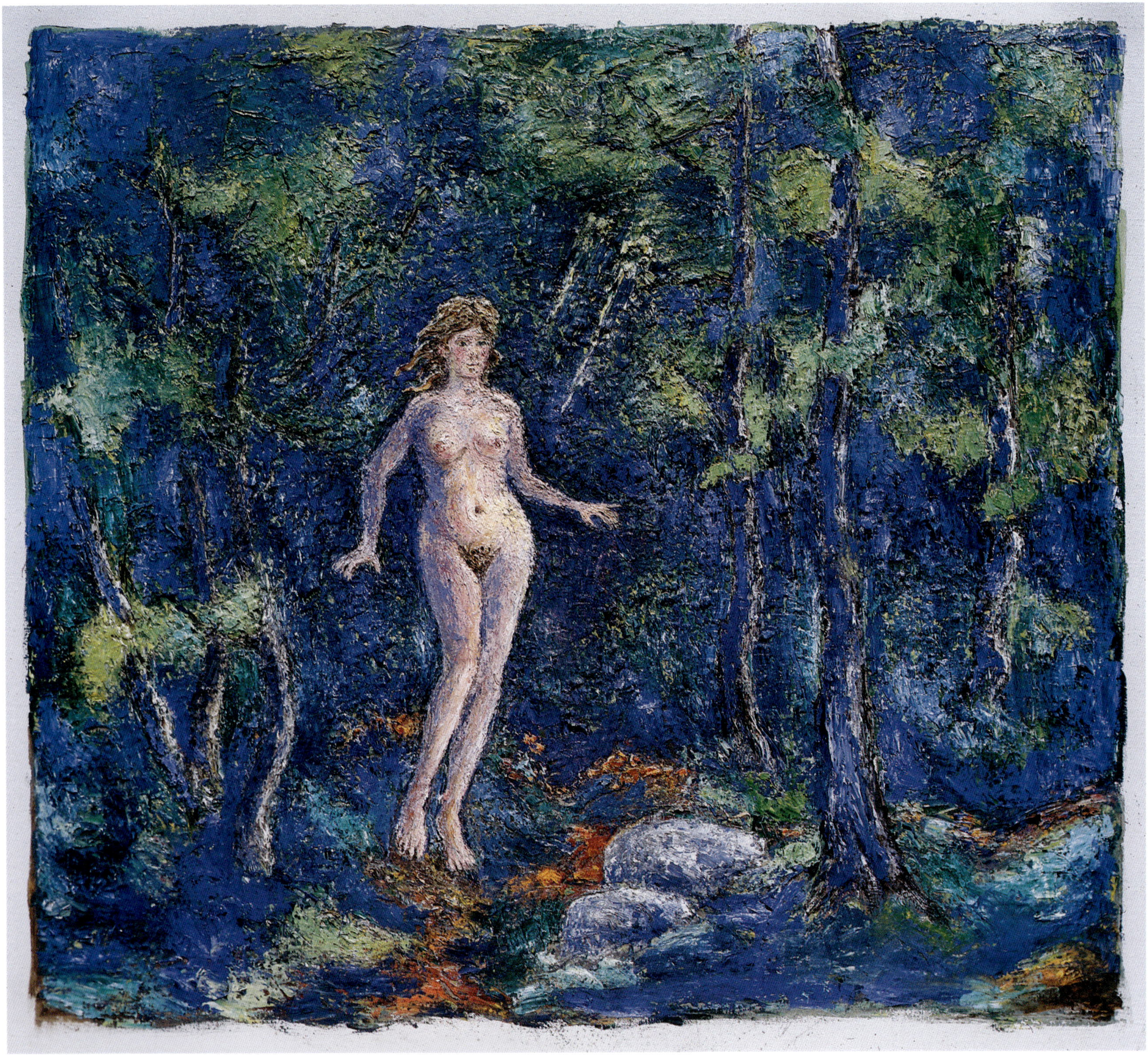

3

O magic sleep! O comfortable bird,
That broodest o'er the troubled sea of the mind
Till it is hush'd and smooth!

Book I 453-455

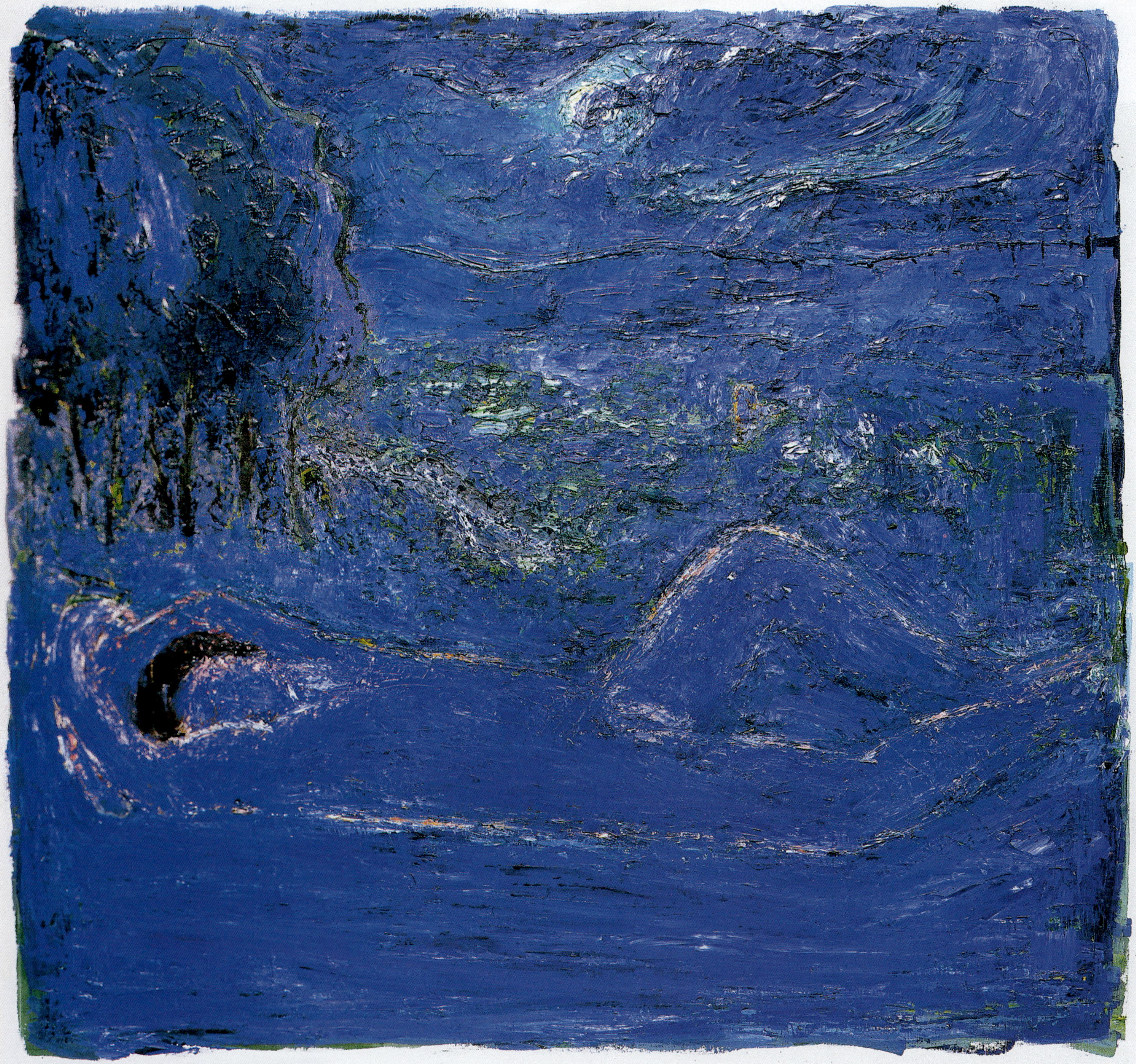

4

Methought I lay
Watching the zenith, where the milky way
Among the stars in virgin splendour pours;
And travelling my eye, until the doors
Of heaven appear'd to open for my flight…

Book I 578-582

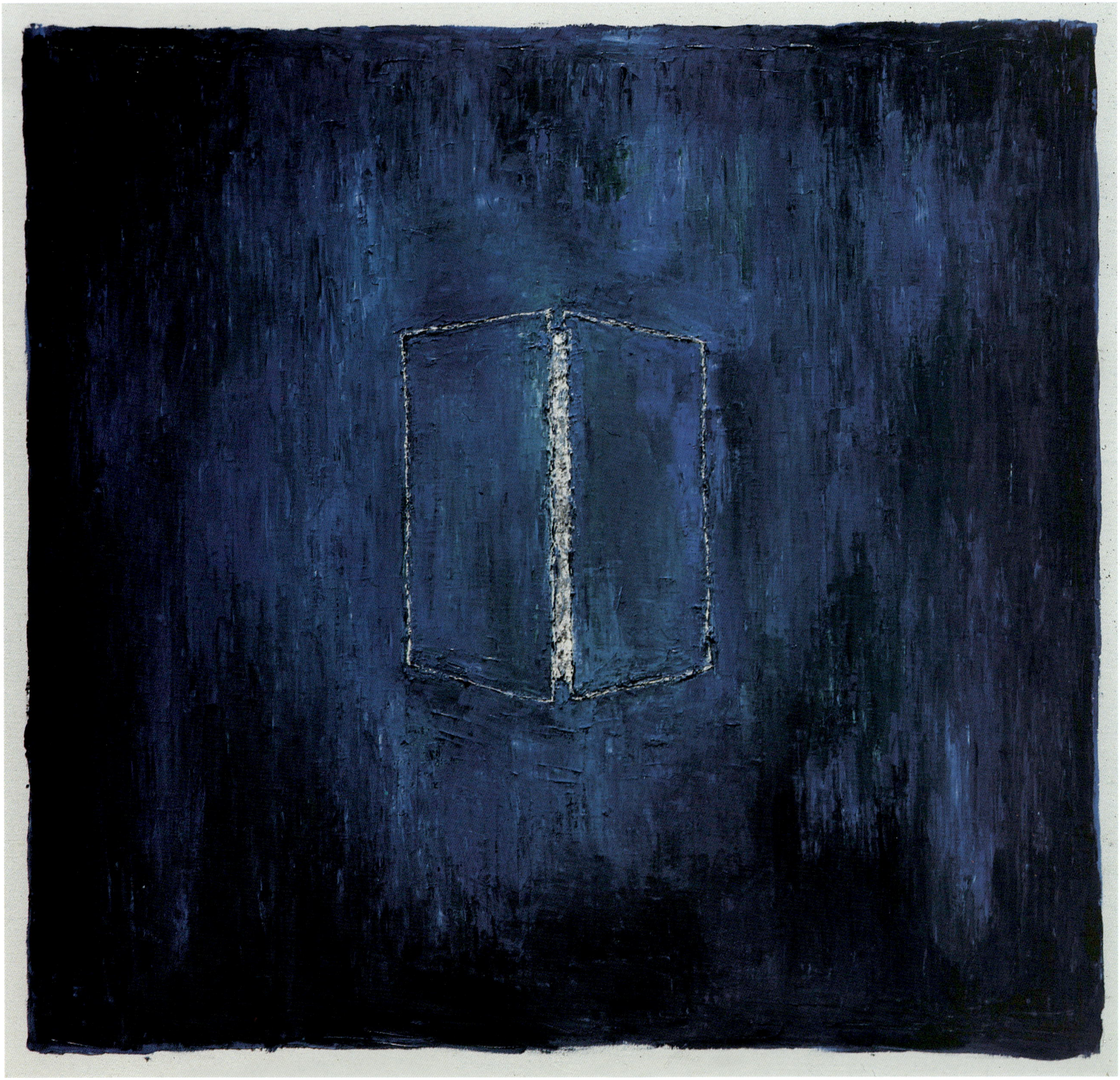

5

And lo! From opening clouds, I saw emerge
The loveliest moon, that ever silver'd o'er
A shell for Neptune's goblet…

Book I 591-593

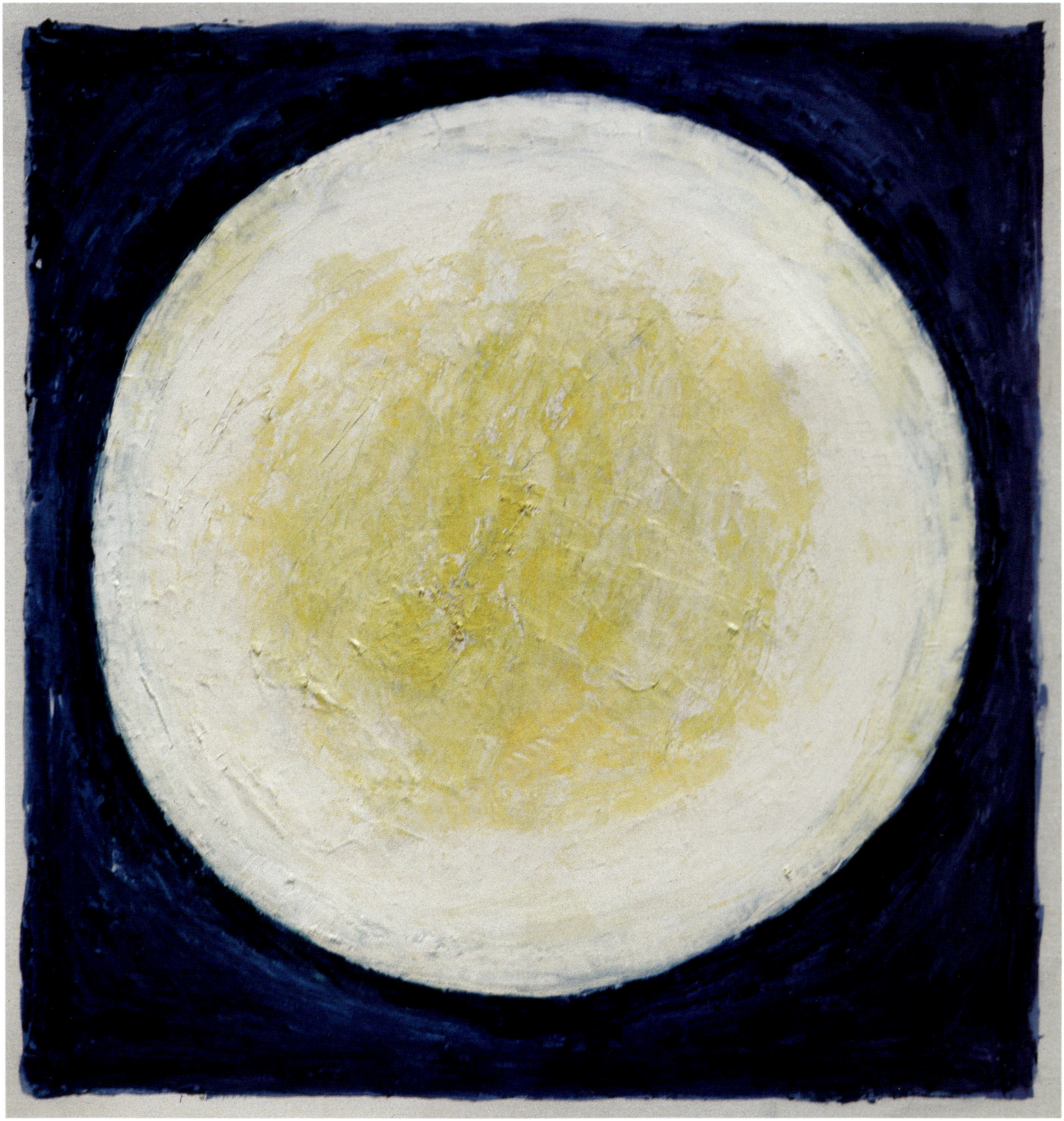

6

On a wide sand they met,
And of those numbers every eye was wet;
For each their old love found. A murmuring rose,
Like what was never heard in all the throes
Of wind and waters: 'tis past human wit
To tell; 'tis dizziness to think of it.

Book III 822-827

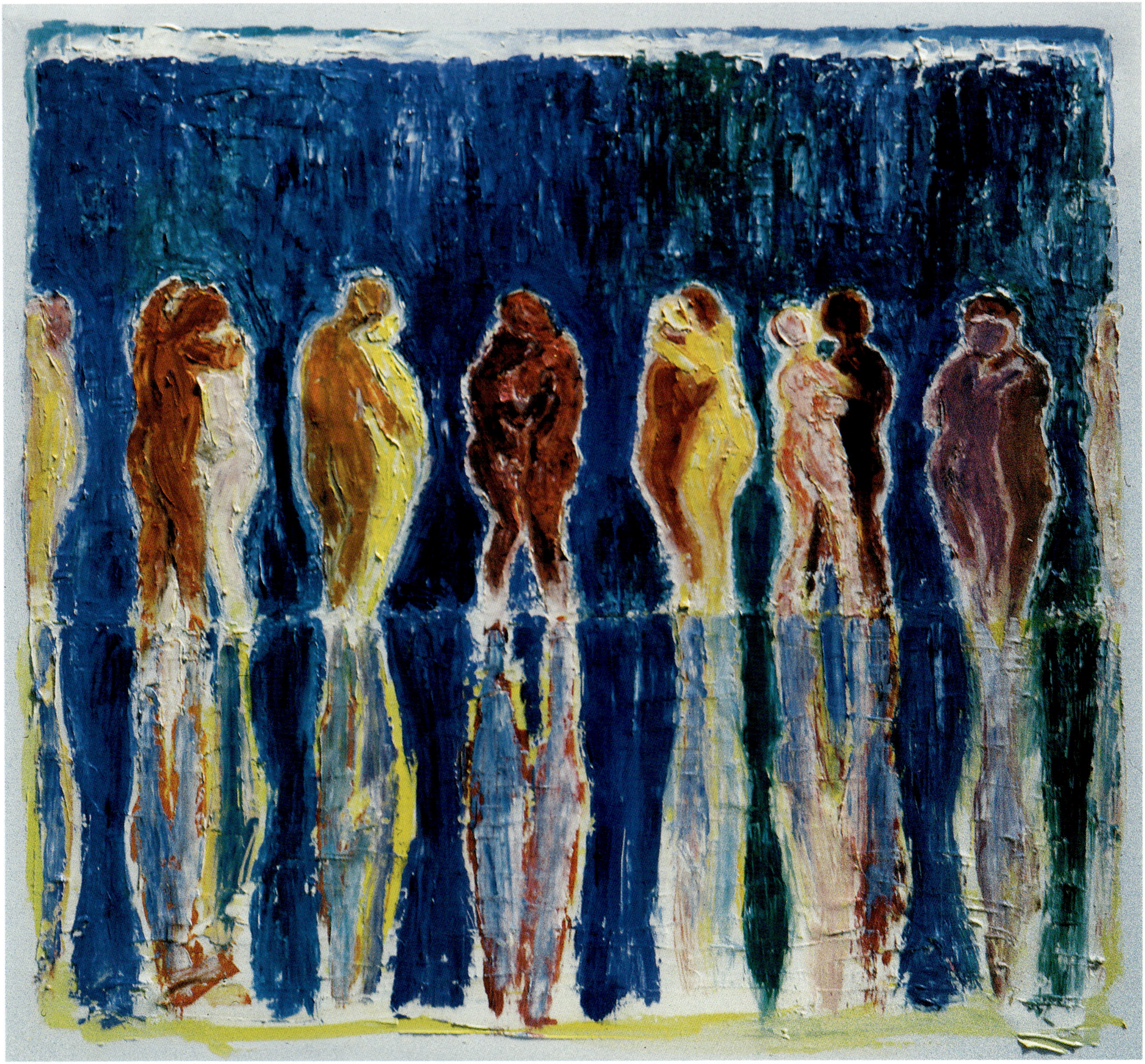

7

Leading the way, young damsels danced along,
Bearing the burden of a shepherd song…

Book I 135-136

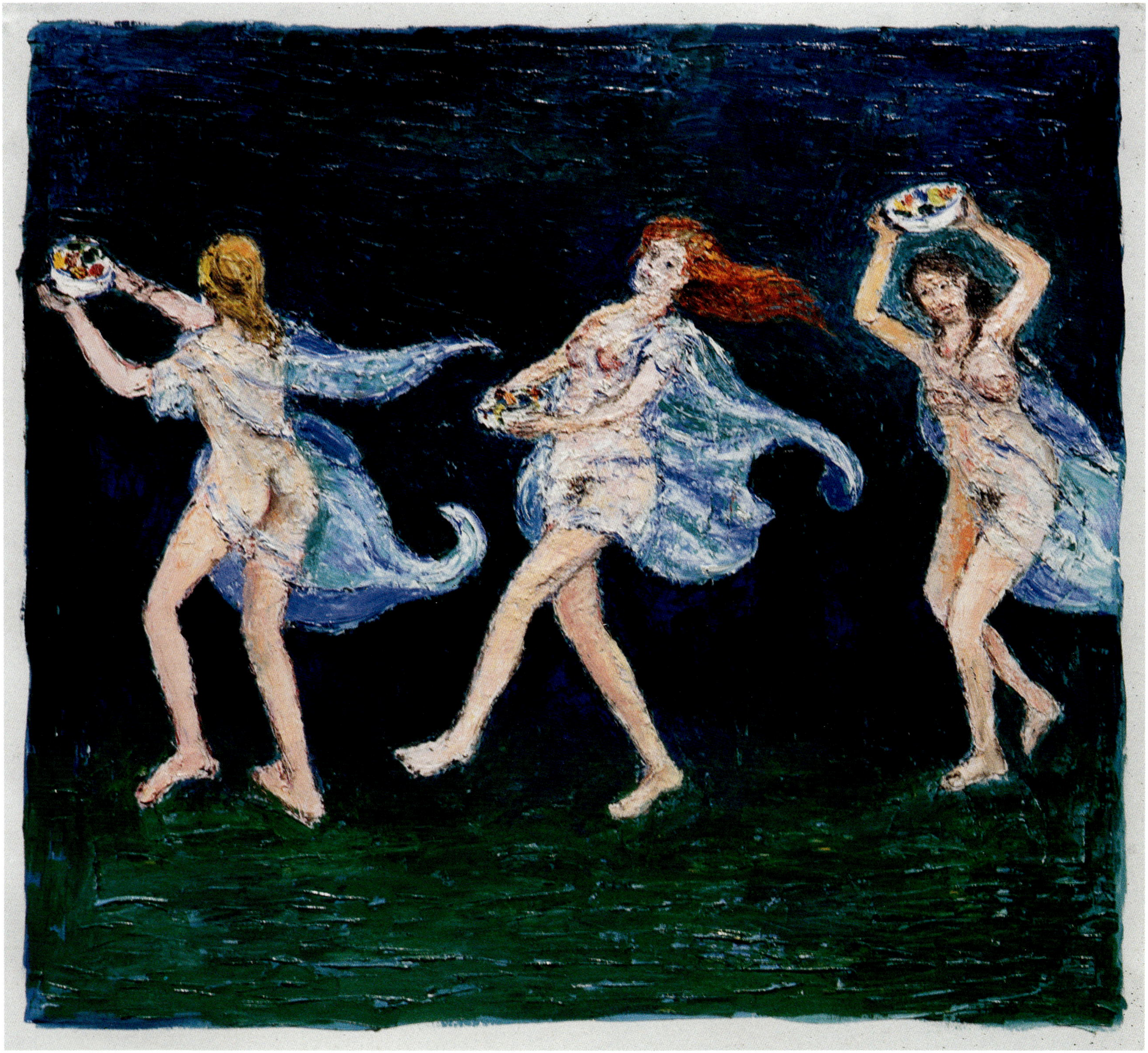

8

Then dance, and song,
And garlanding grew wild; and pleasure reign'd.
In harmless tendril they each other chain'd,
And strove who should be smother'd deepest in
Fresh crush of leaves.

Book III 933-937

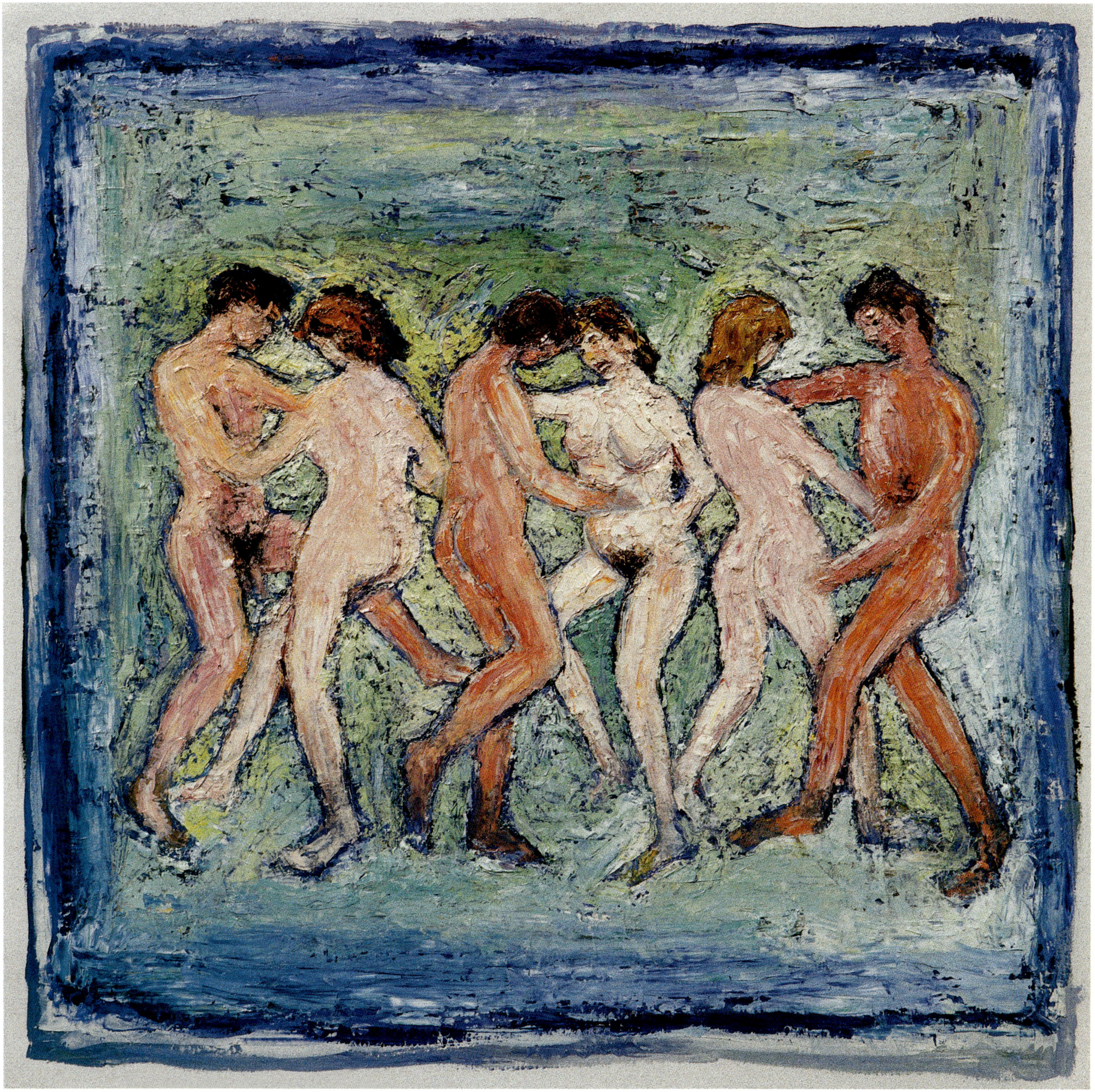

9

These lovers did embrace, and we must weep
That there is no power left to steep
A quill immortal in these joyous tears…

Book II 730-732

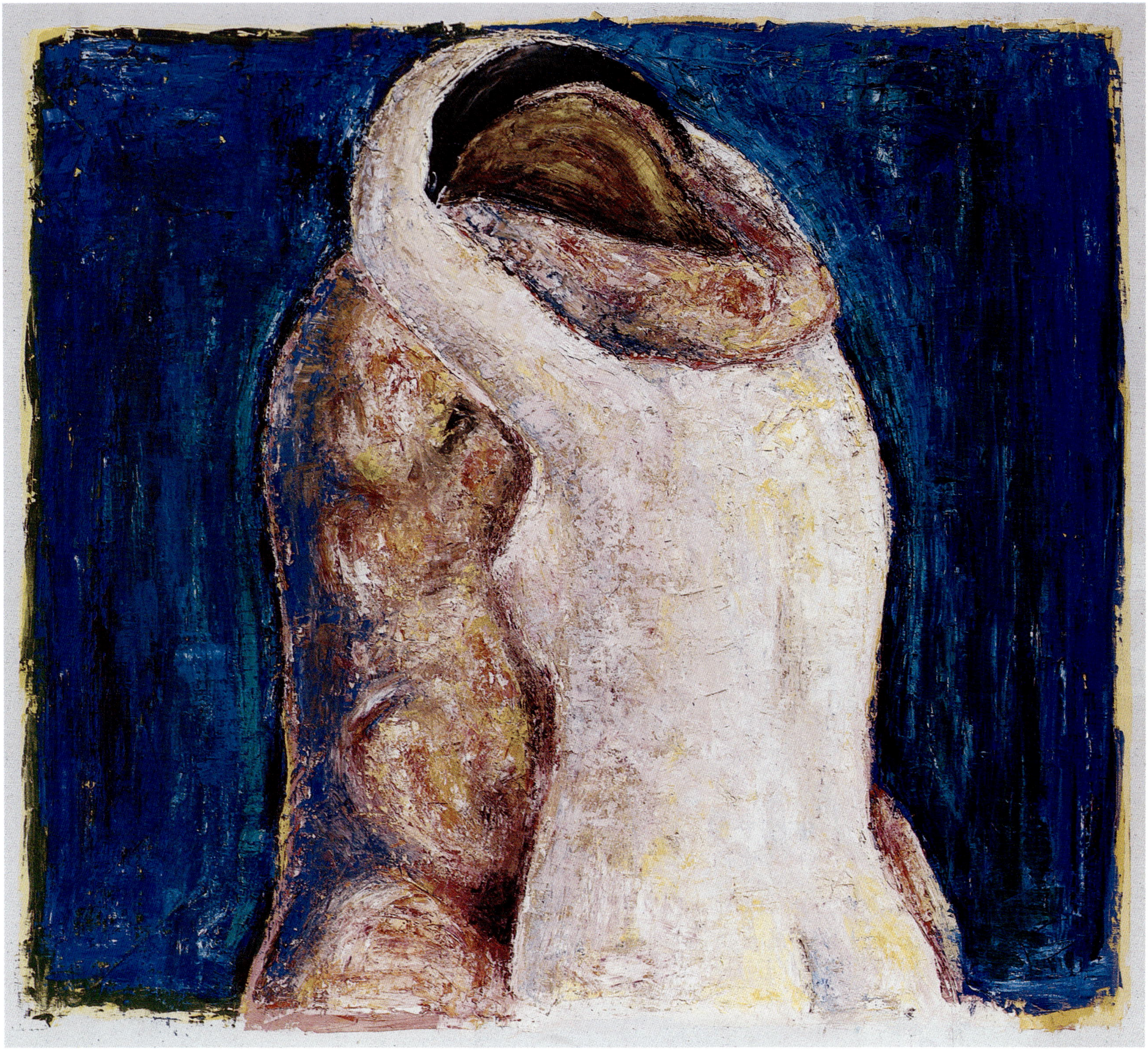

10

O sweetest essence! sweetest of all minions!
God of warm pulses, and dishevell'd hair,
And panting bosoms bare!

Book III 983-985

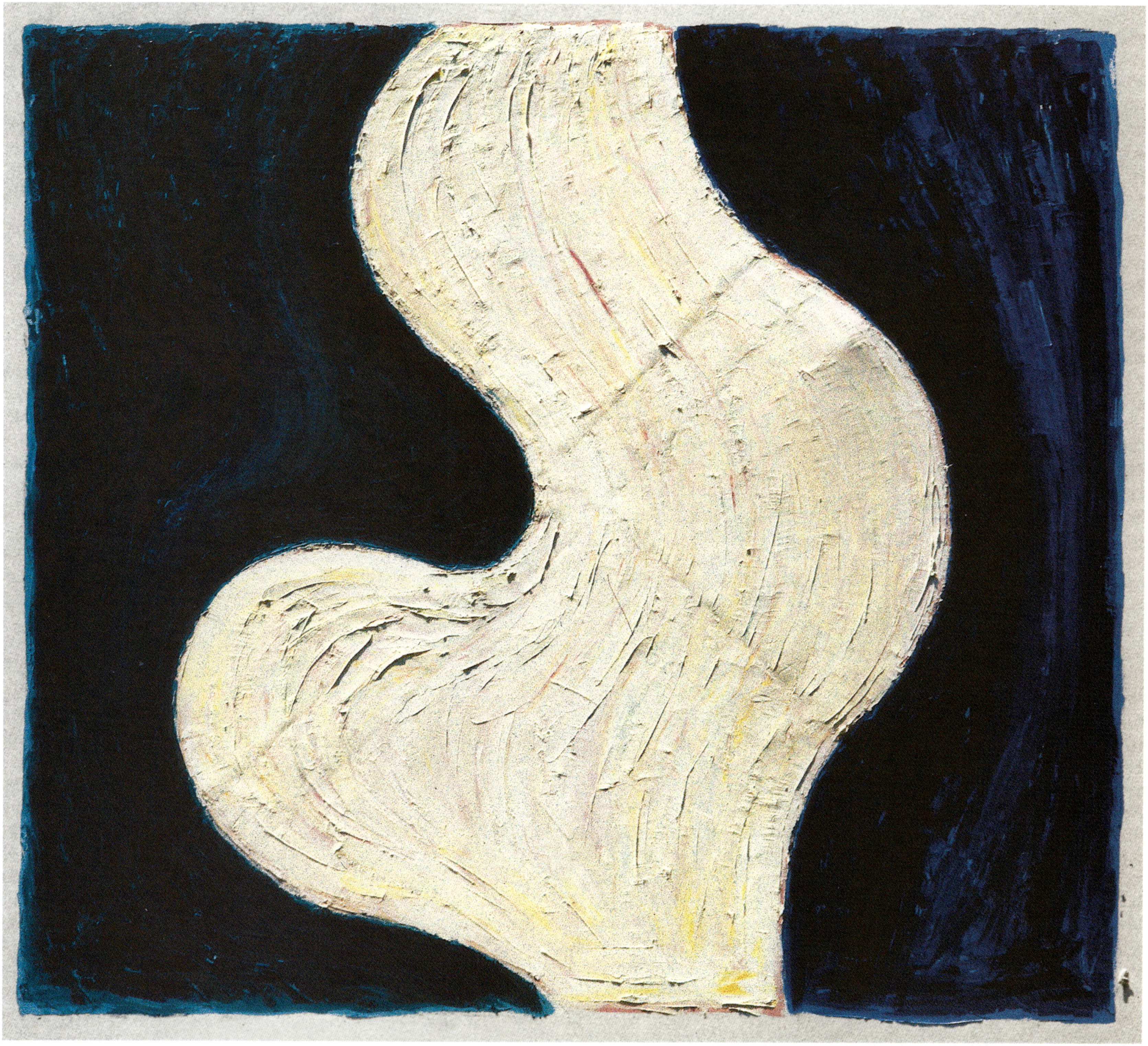

11

O ye deities,
Who from Olympus watch our destinies!
Whence that completed form of all completeness?
Whence came that high perfection of all sweetness?

Book I 605-607

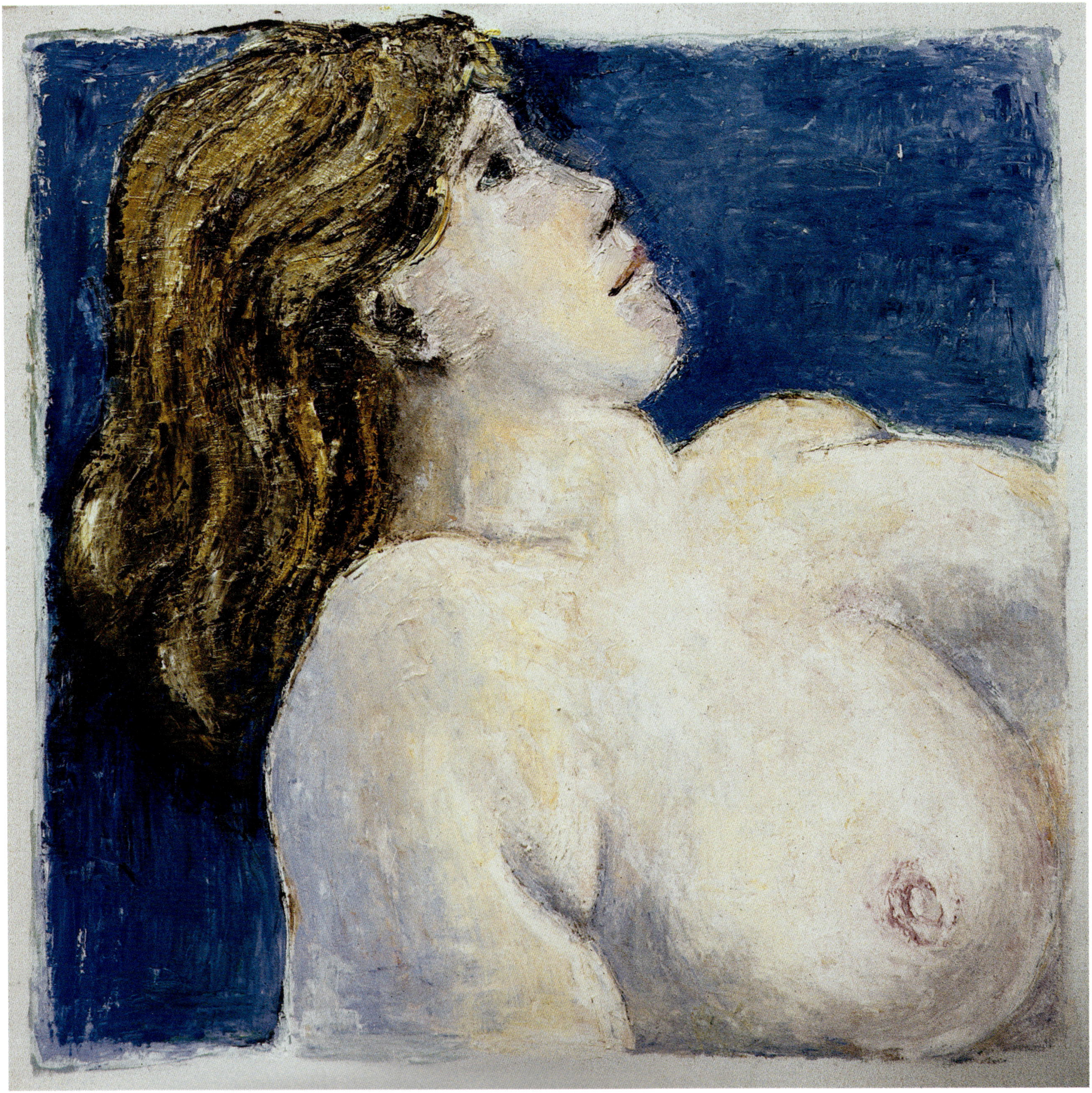

12

Who could resist? Who in this universe?
She did so breathe ambrosia; so immerse
My fine existence in a golden clime.
She took me like a child of suckling time,
And cradled me in roses.

Book III 453-457

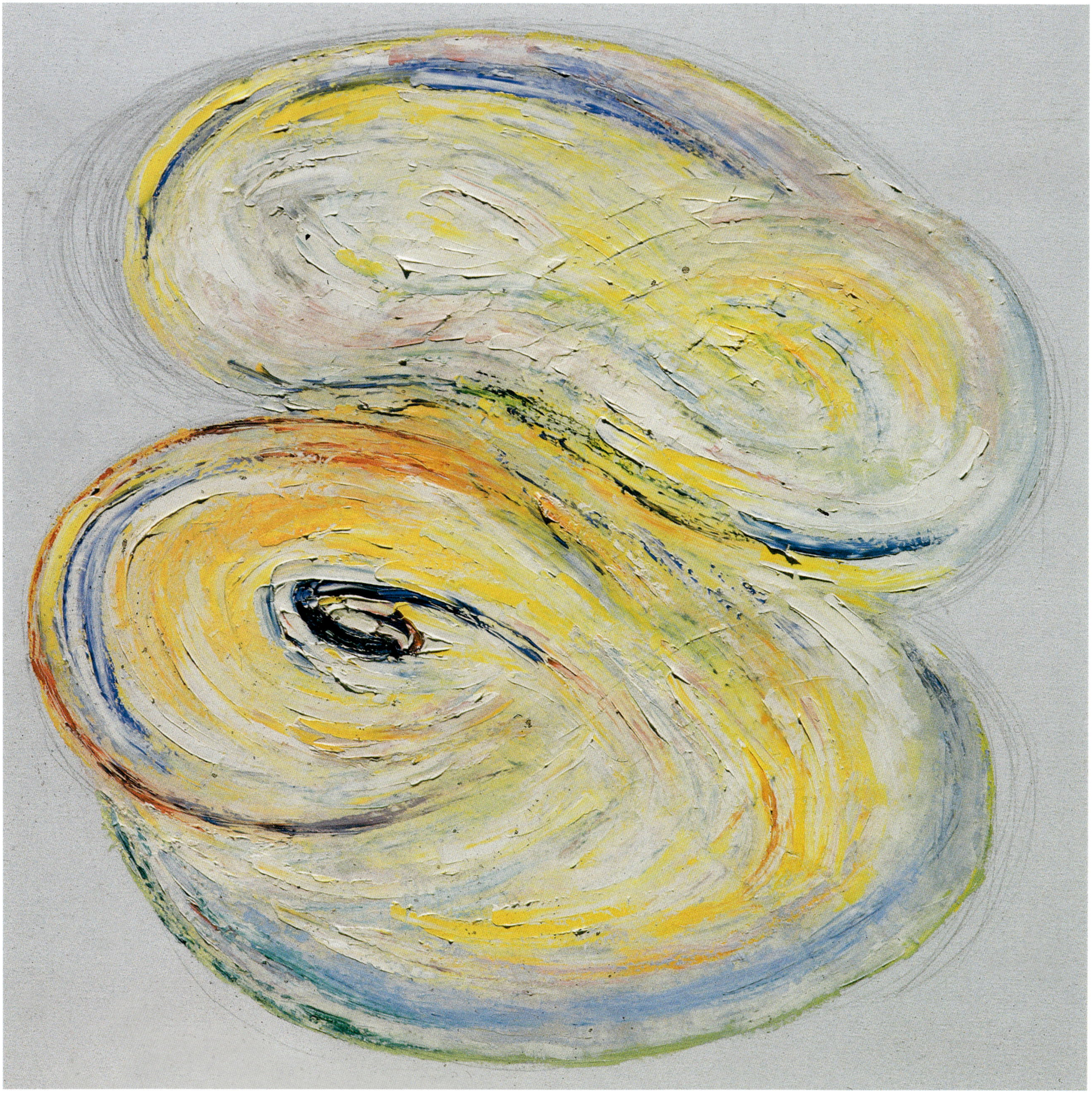

13

...if thou wilt behold all beauty's store,

Behold her panting in the forest grass!

Book IV 58-59

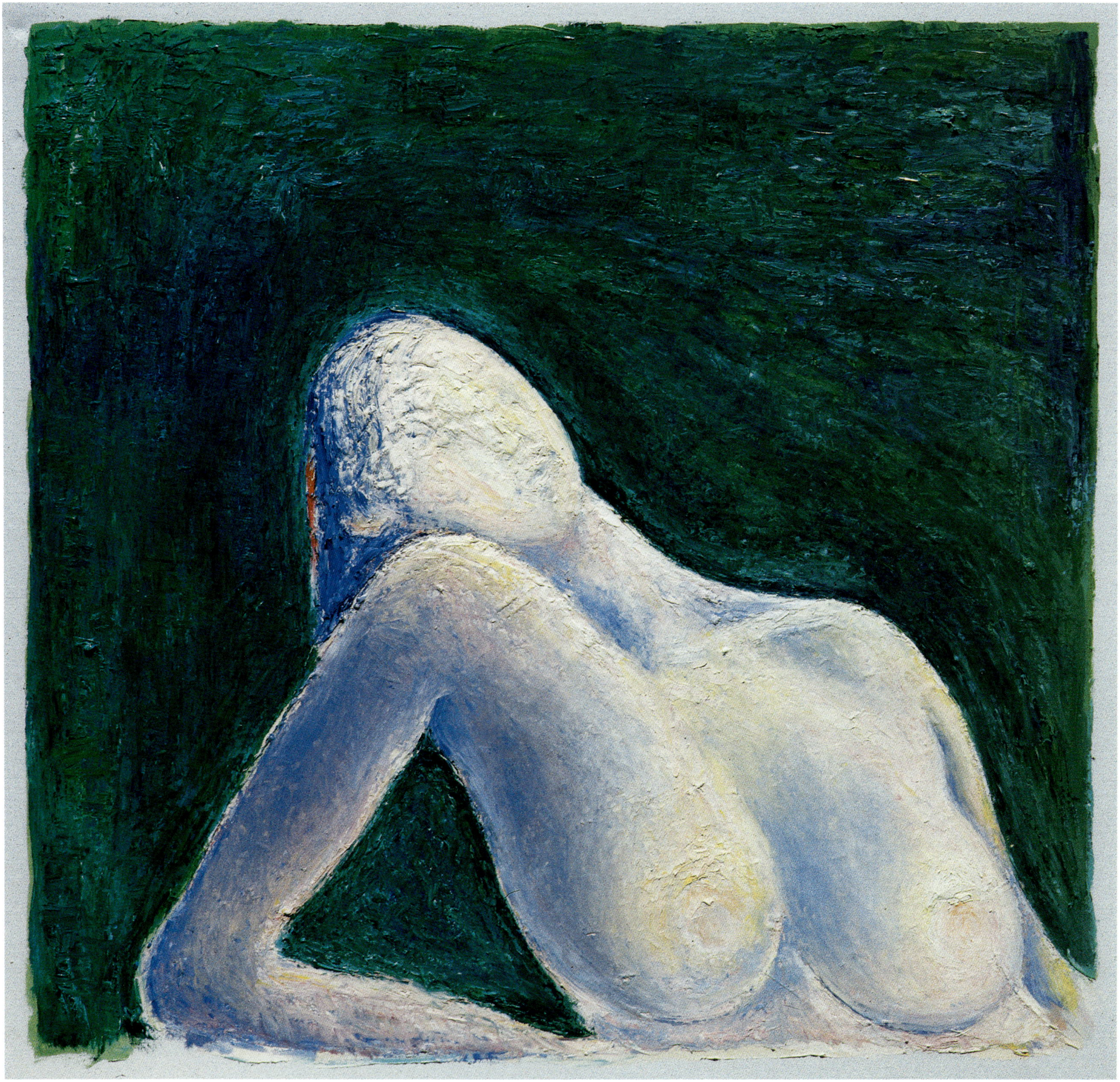

14

...there she lay,
Sweet as a muskrose upon new-made hay;
With all her limbs on tremble...

Book IV   101-103

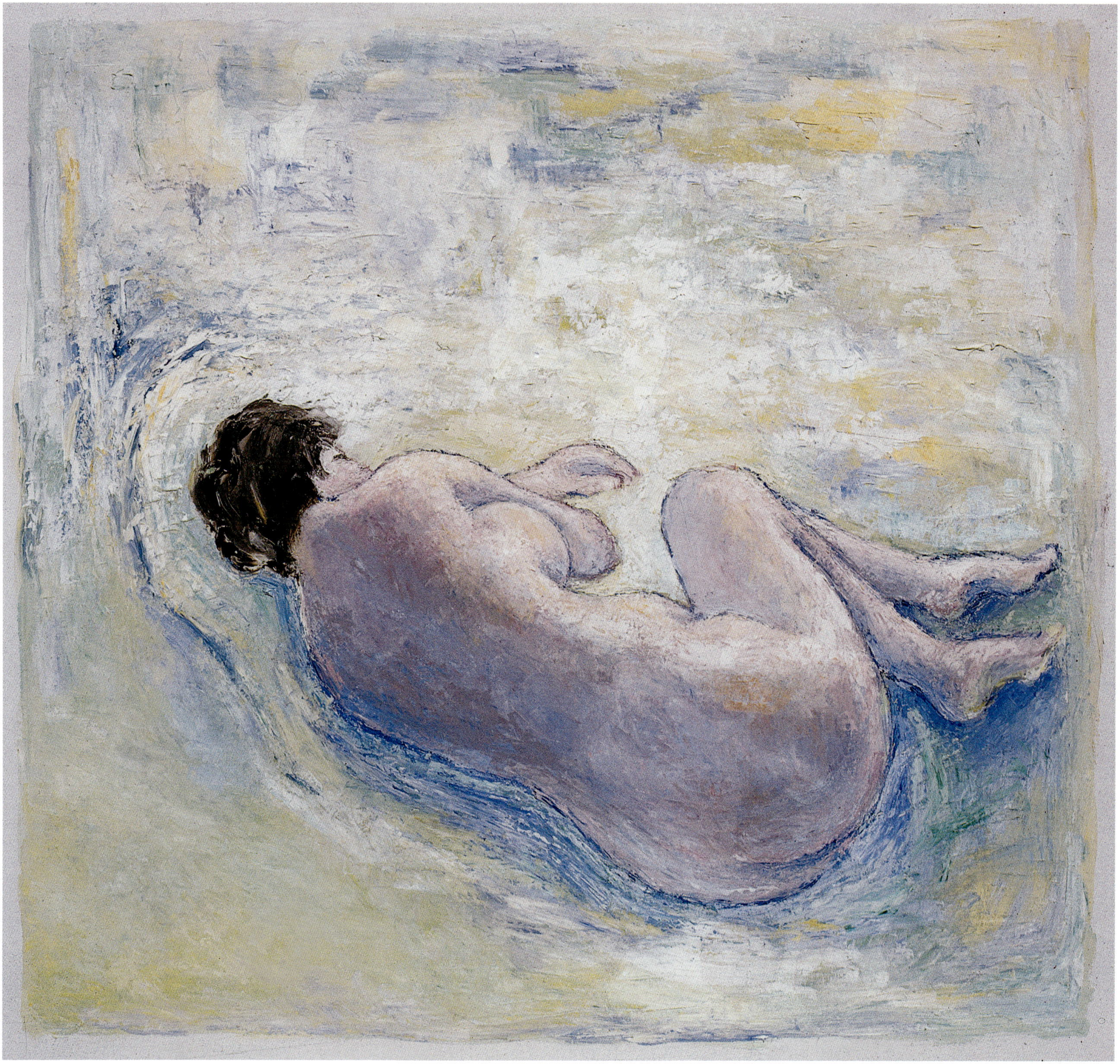

15

With tears, and smiles, and honey-words she wove
A net whose thraldom was more bliss than all
The range of flower'd Elysium.

Book III 426–428

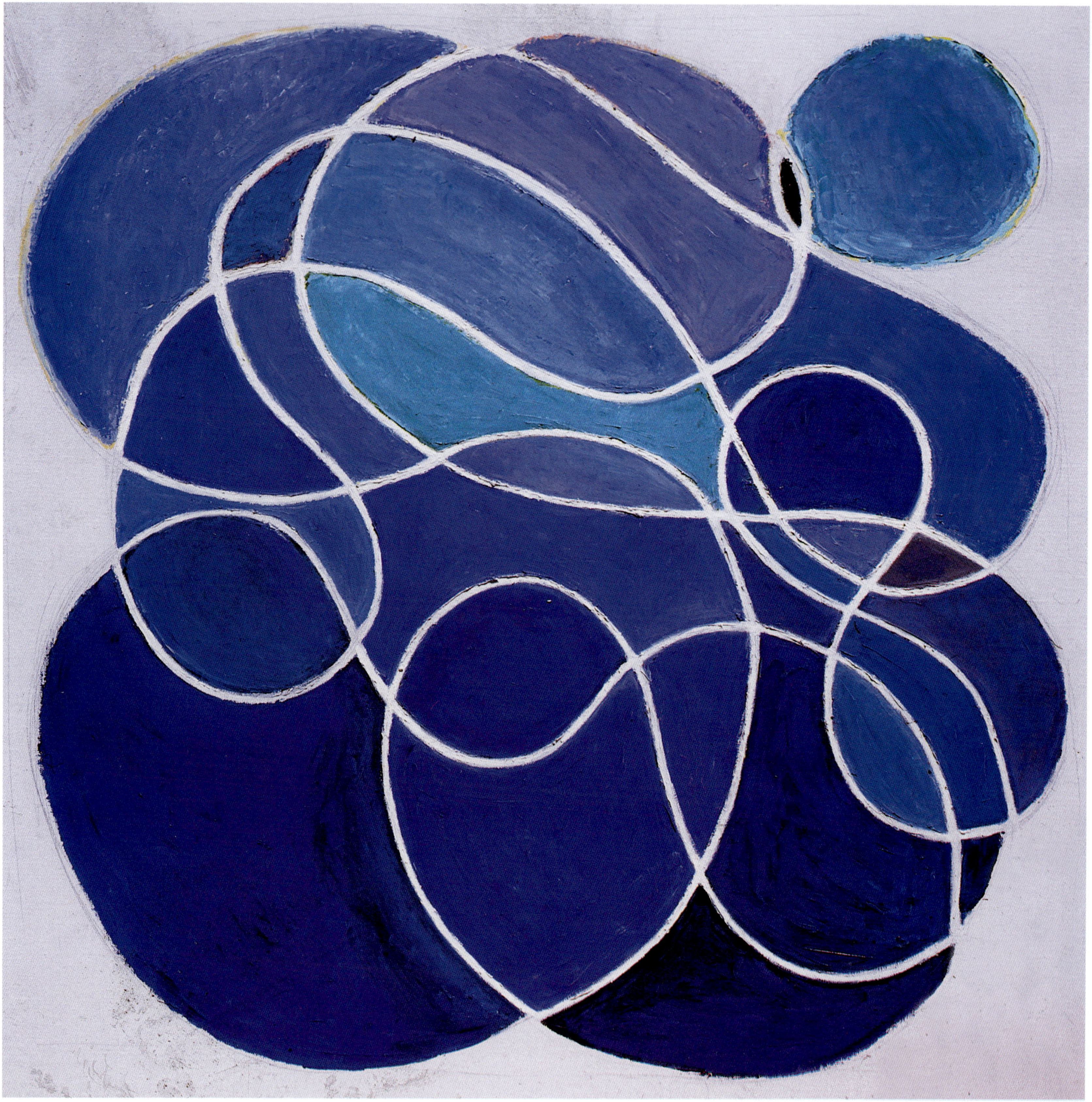

16

...towards me, like a very maid,
Came blushing, waning, willing, and afraid...

Book I 634-635

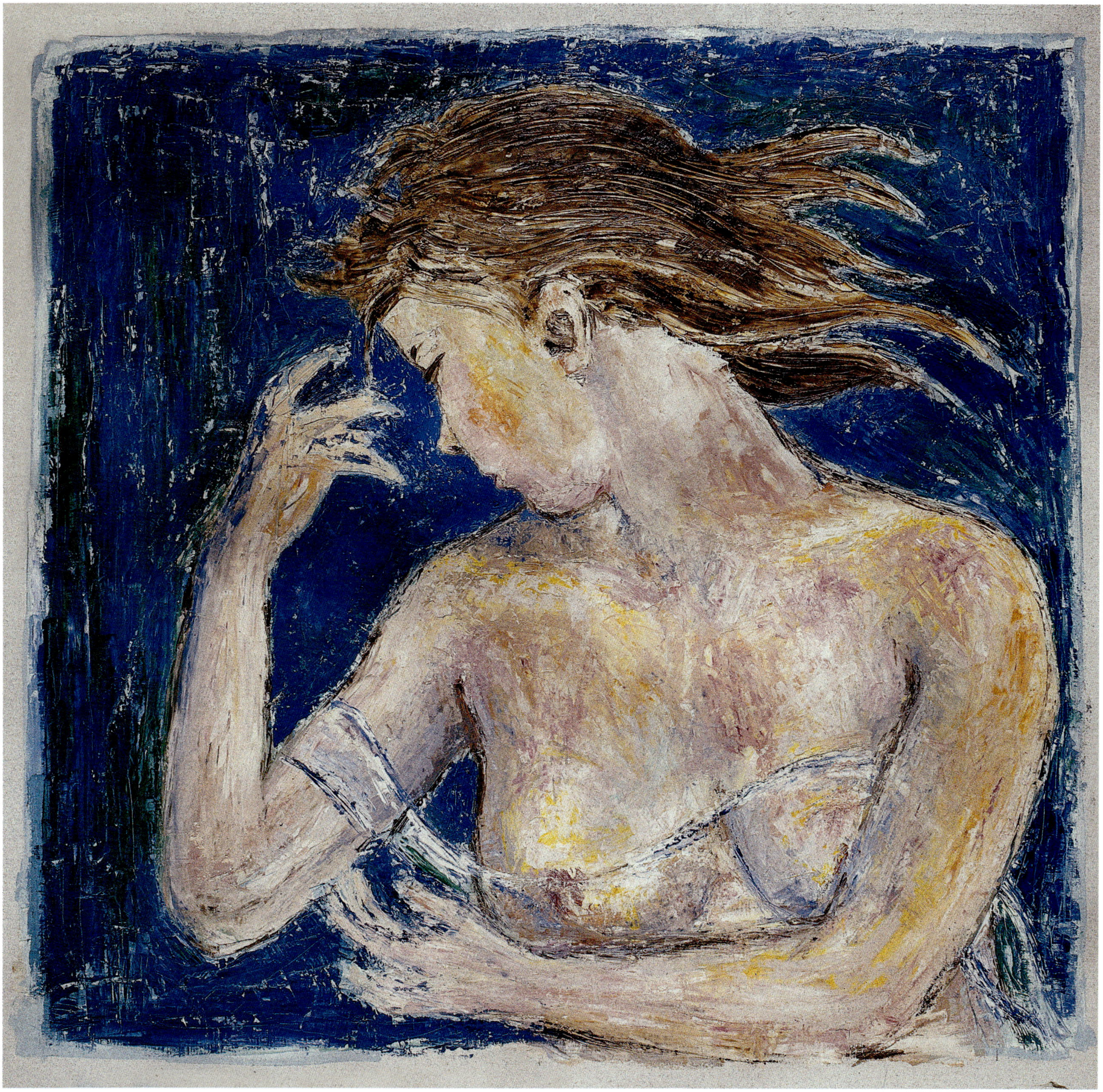

17

It was a nymph uprisen to the breast
In the fountain's pebbly margin…

Book II 98-99

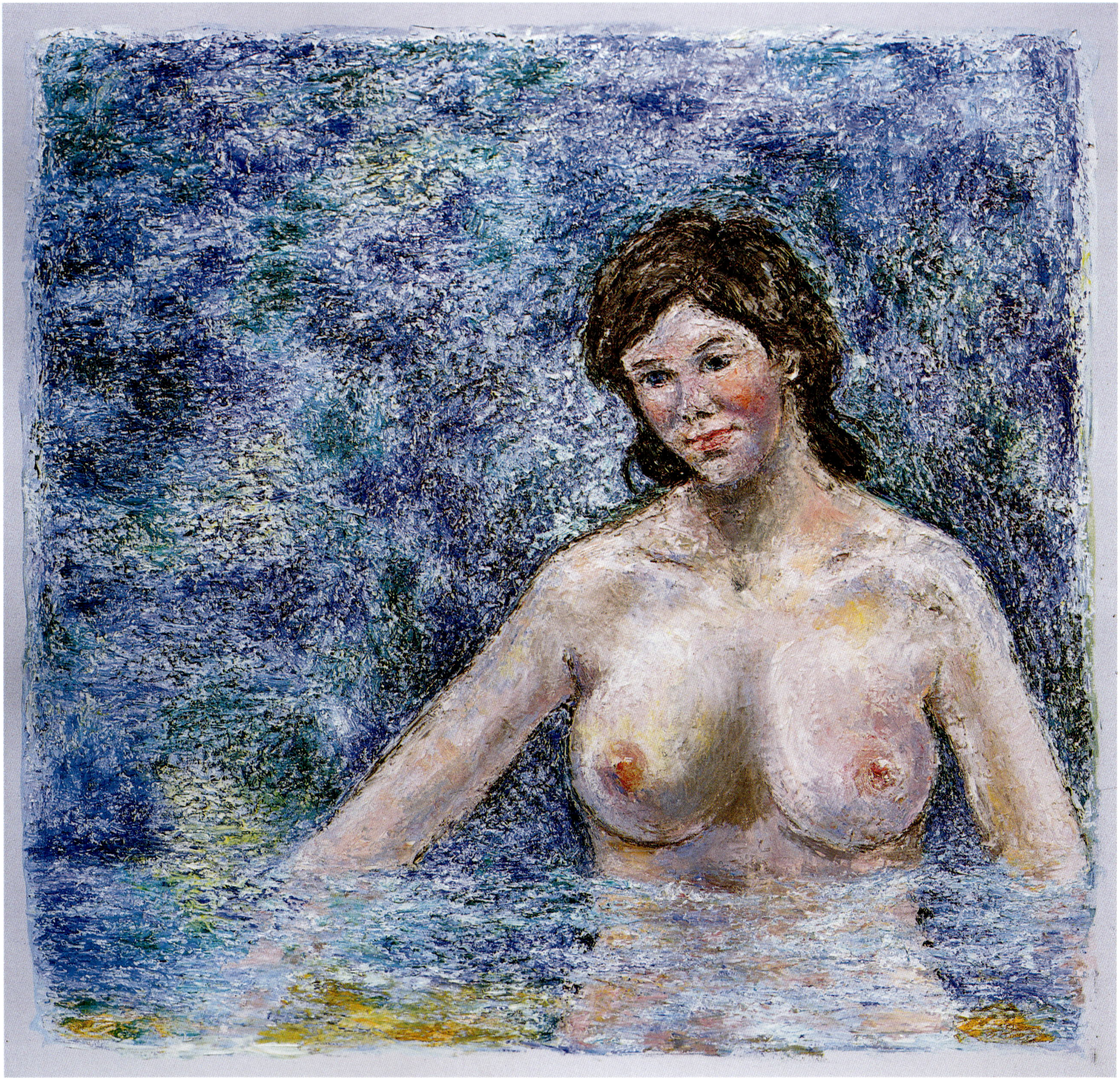

18

...O bliss!

A naked waist...

Book II 712-713

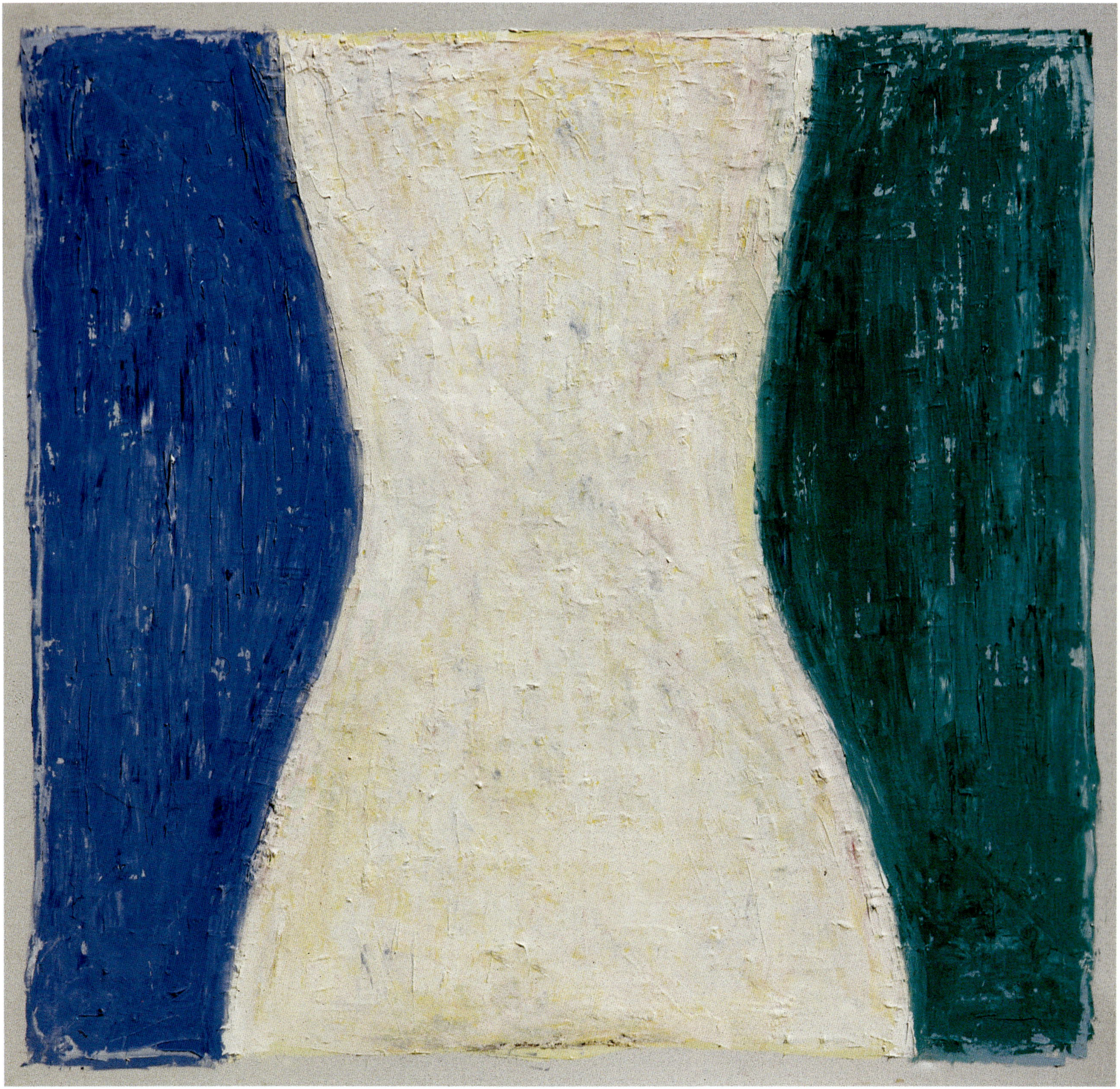

19

Ah! see her hovering feet,
More bluely vein'd, more soft, more whitely sweet
Than those of sea-born Venus, when she rose
From out her cradle shell.

Book I 624-627

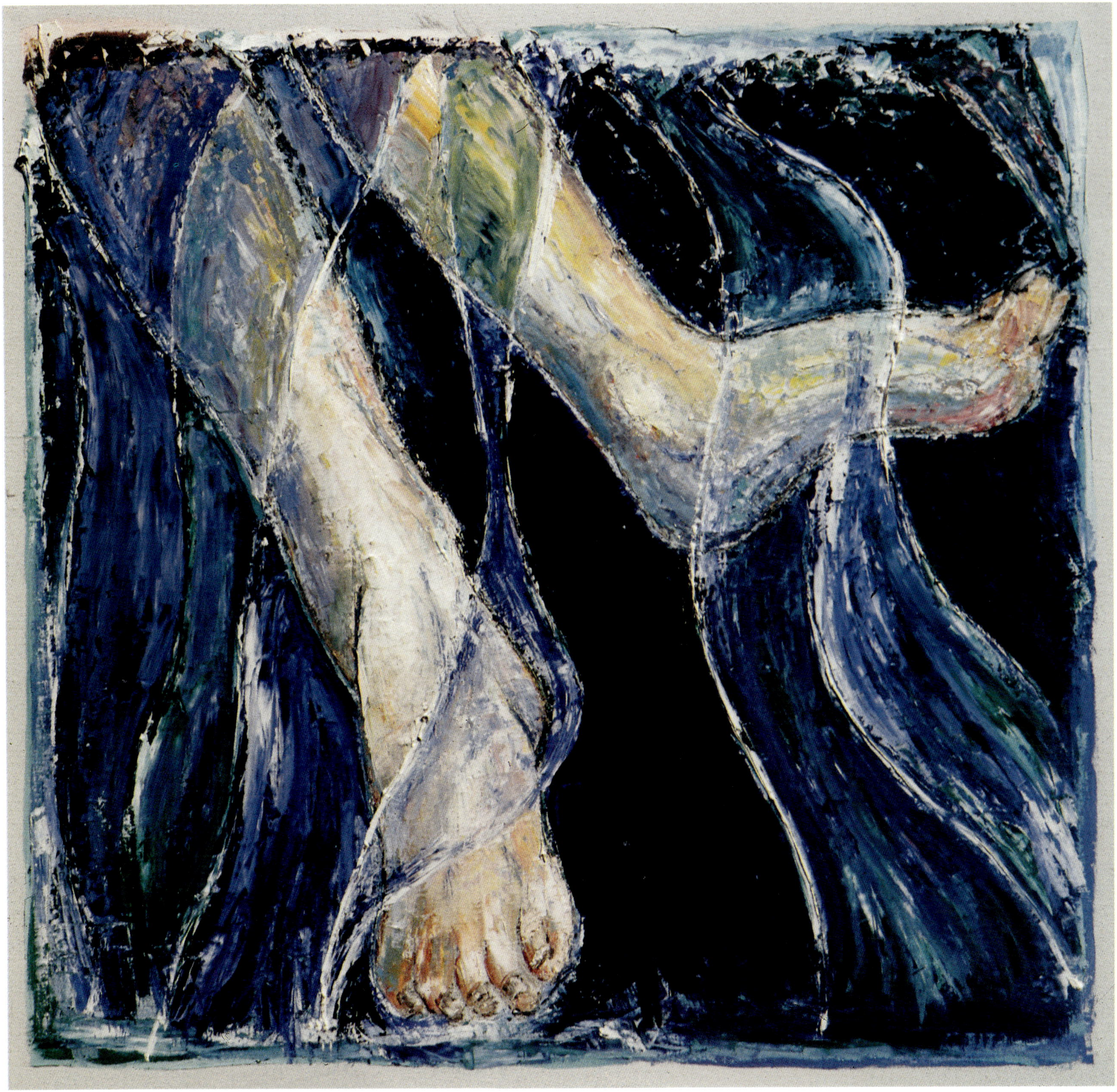

20

My passion grew

The more, the more I saw her dainty hue

Gleam delicately through the azure clear…

Book III 407-409

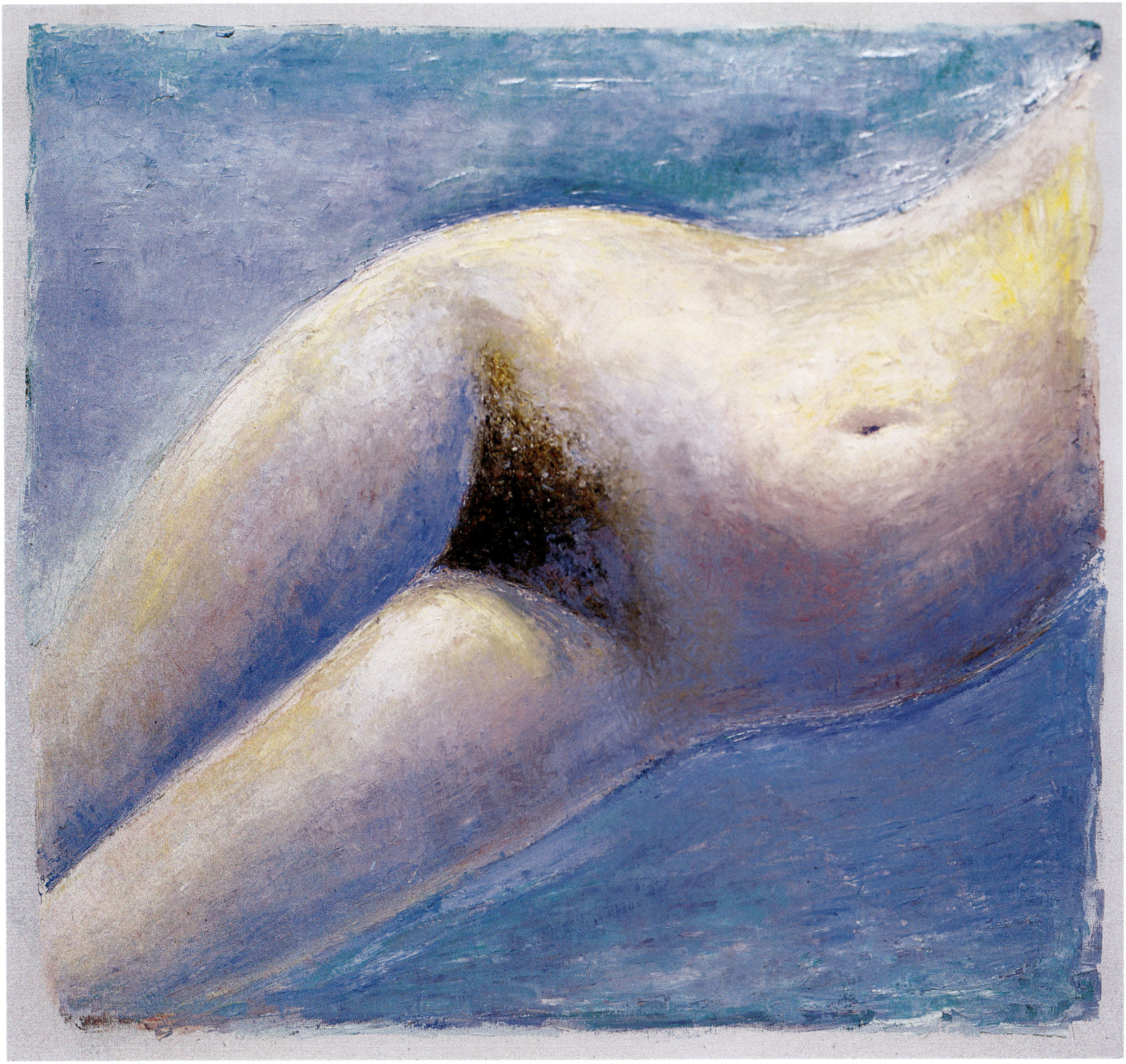

21

O that her shining hair was in the sun,
And I distilling from it thence to run
In amorous rillets down her shrinking form!
To linger on her lily shoulders, warm
Between her kissing breasts, and every charm
Touch raptur'd!

Book II 943-948

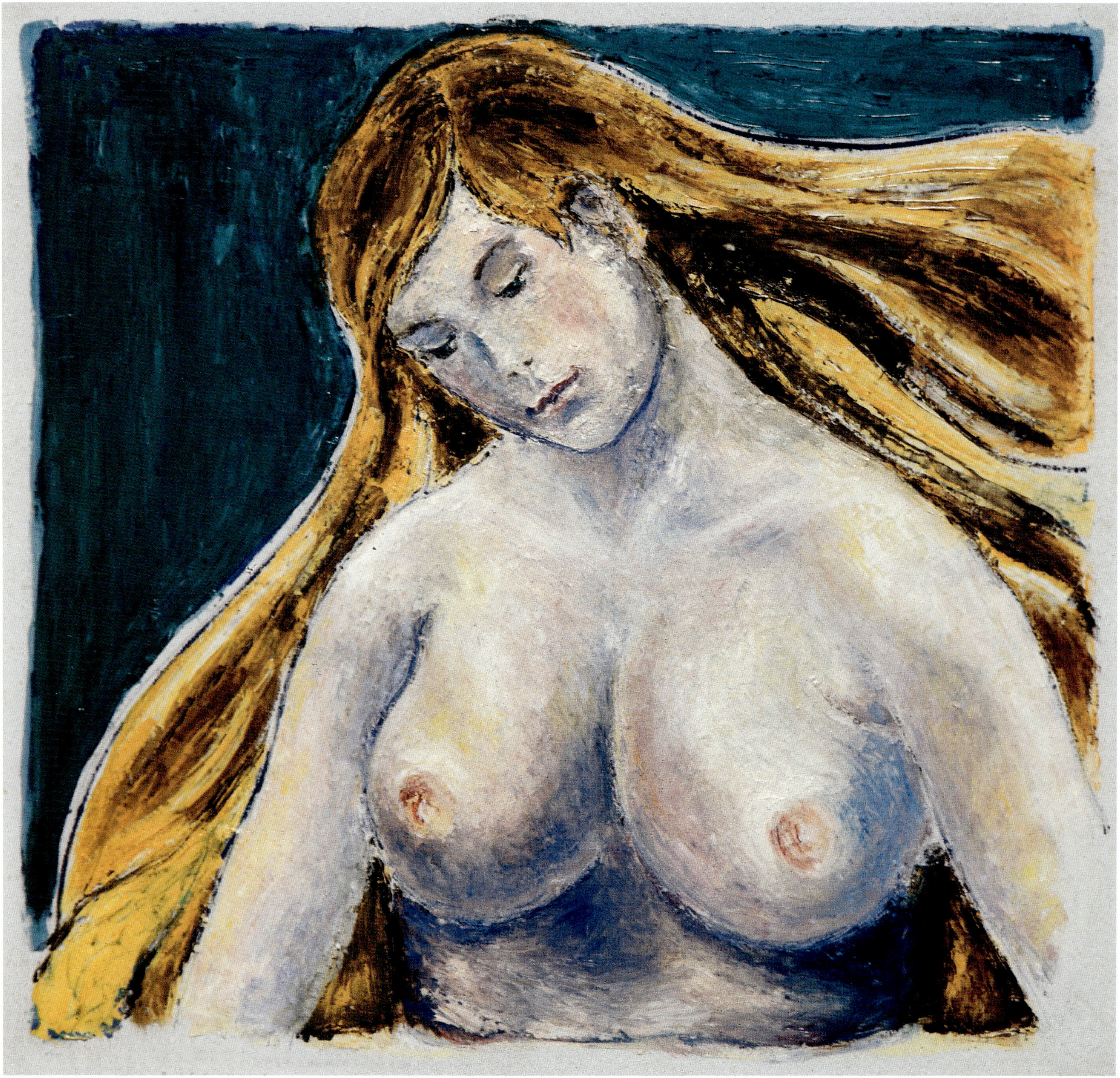

22

...Let me dive into the joy I seek...

Book IV 690

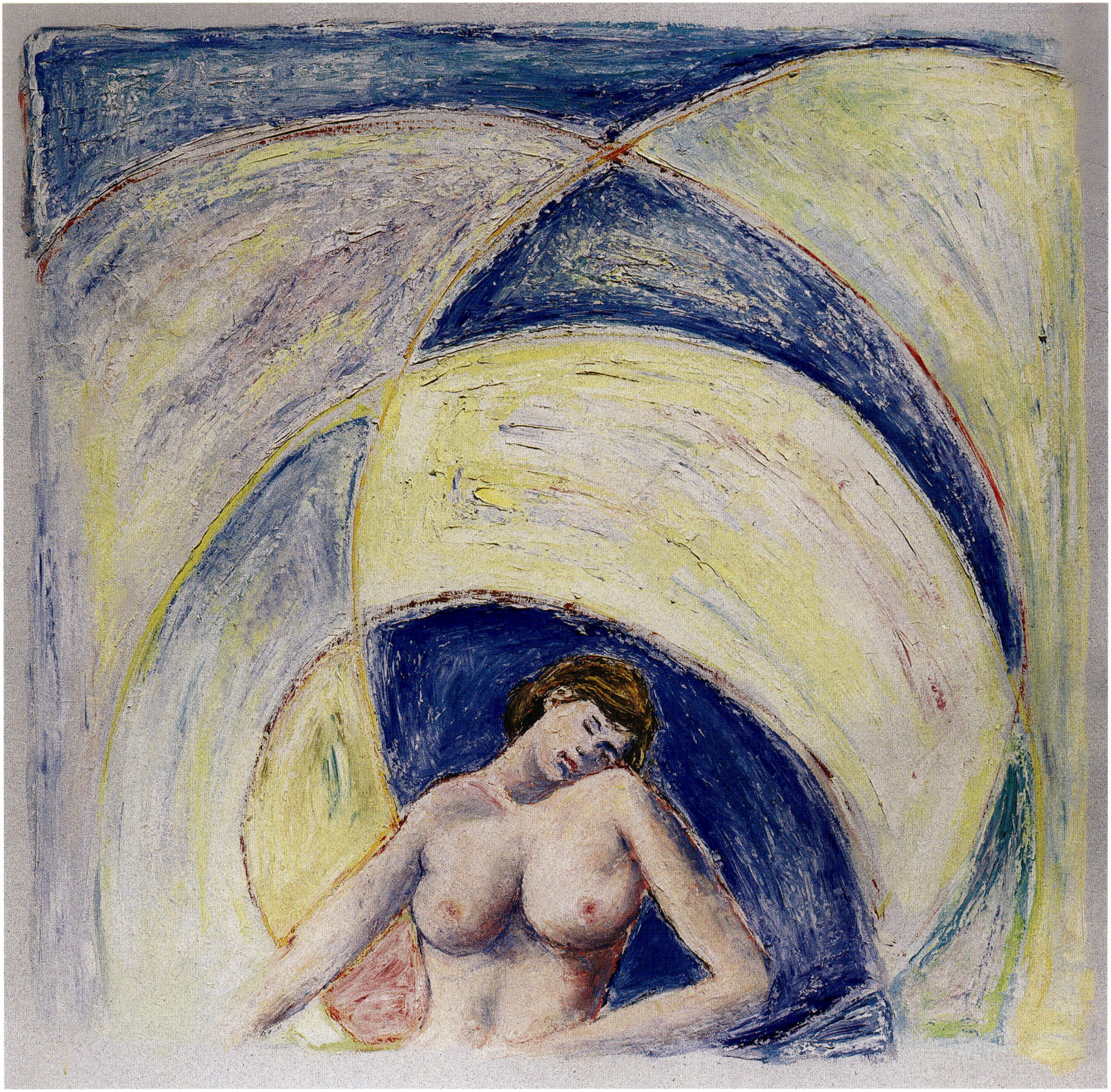

23

With such a paradise of lips and eyes,
Blush-tinted cheeks, half smiles, and faintest sighs…

Book I 621-622

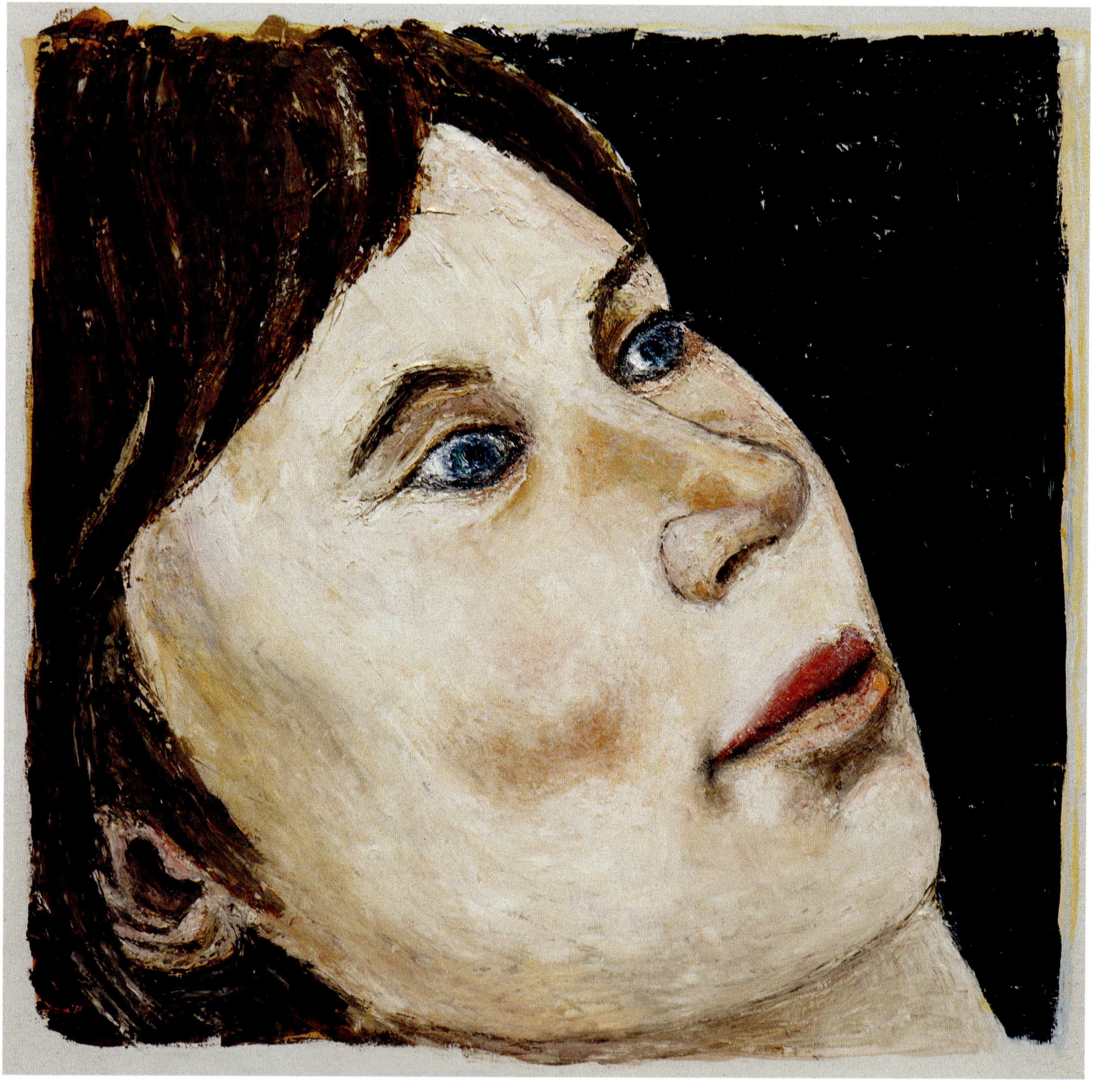

24

I lov'd her to the very white of truth…

Book III 402

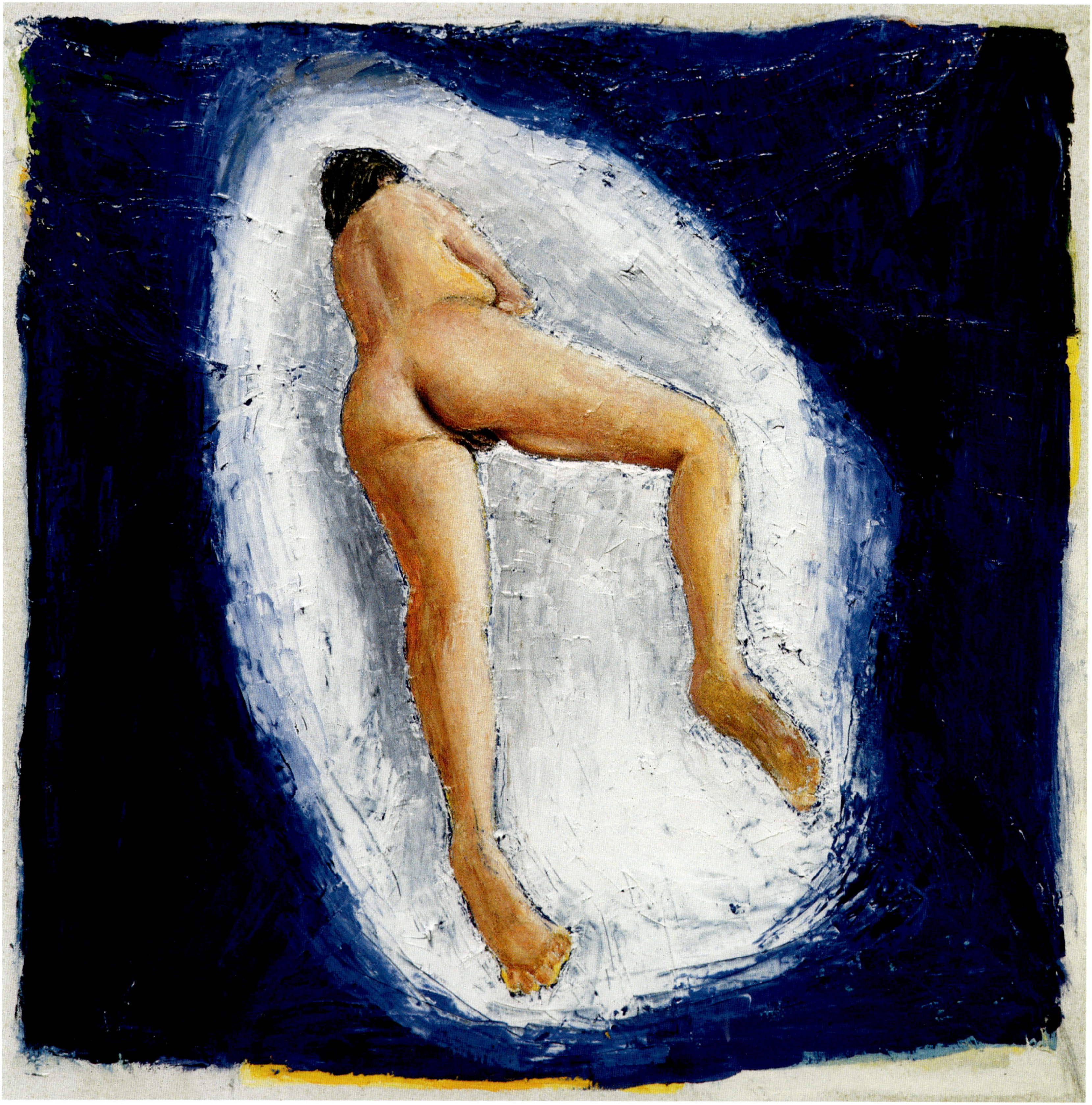

25

Her soft arms were entwining me, and on
Her voice I hung like fruit among green leaves:
Her lips were all my own, and – ah, ripe sheaves
Of happiness!

Book III 270-273

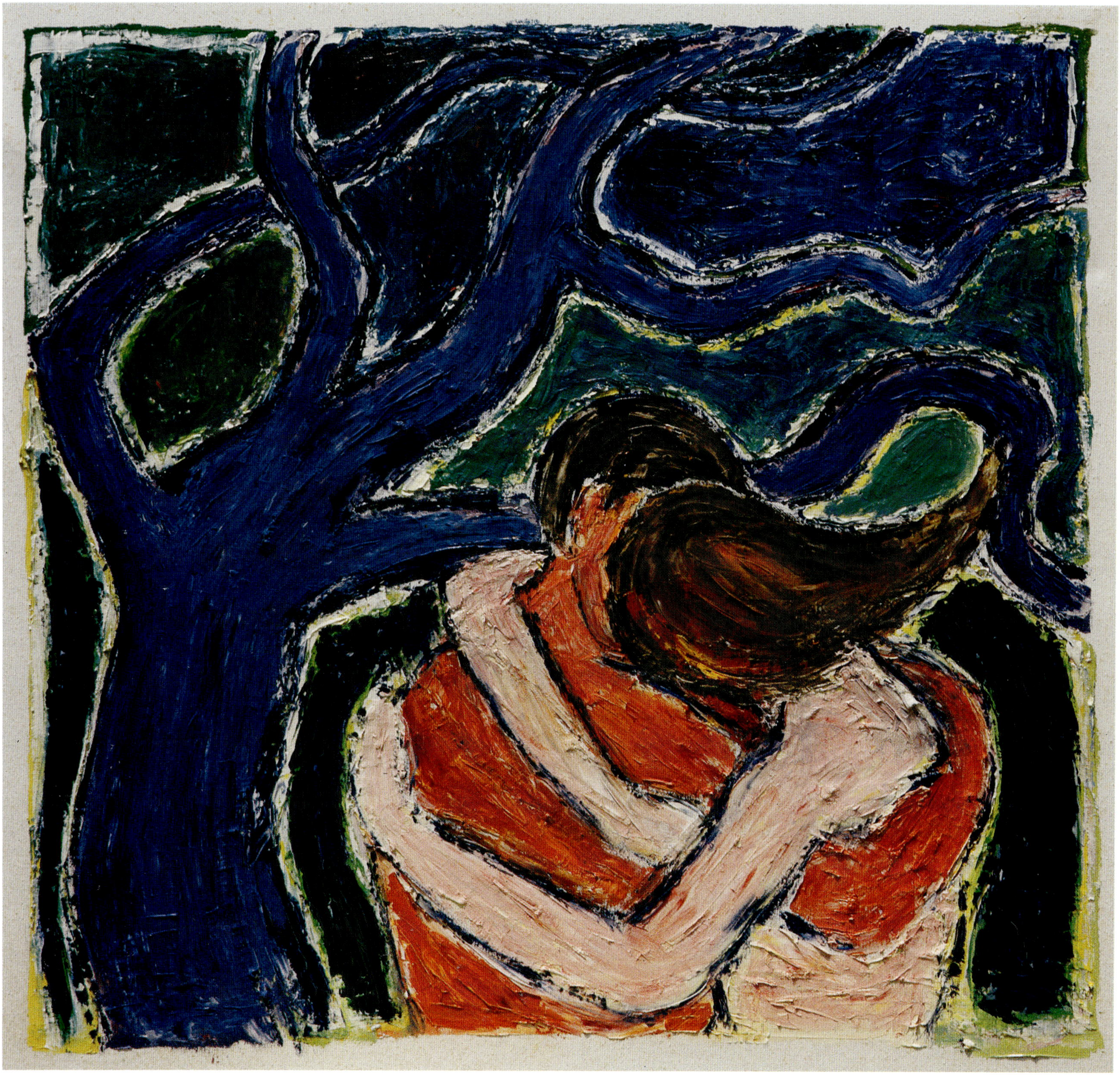

26

I even dared to press
Her very cheek against my crowned lip…

Book I 661-662

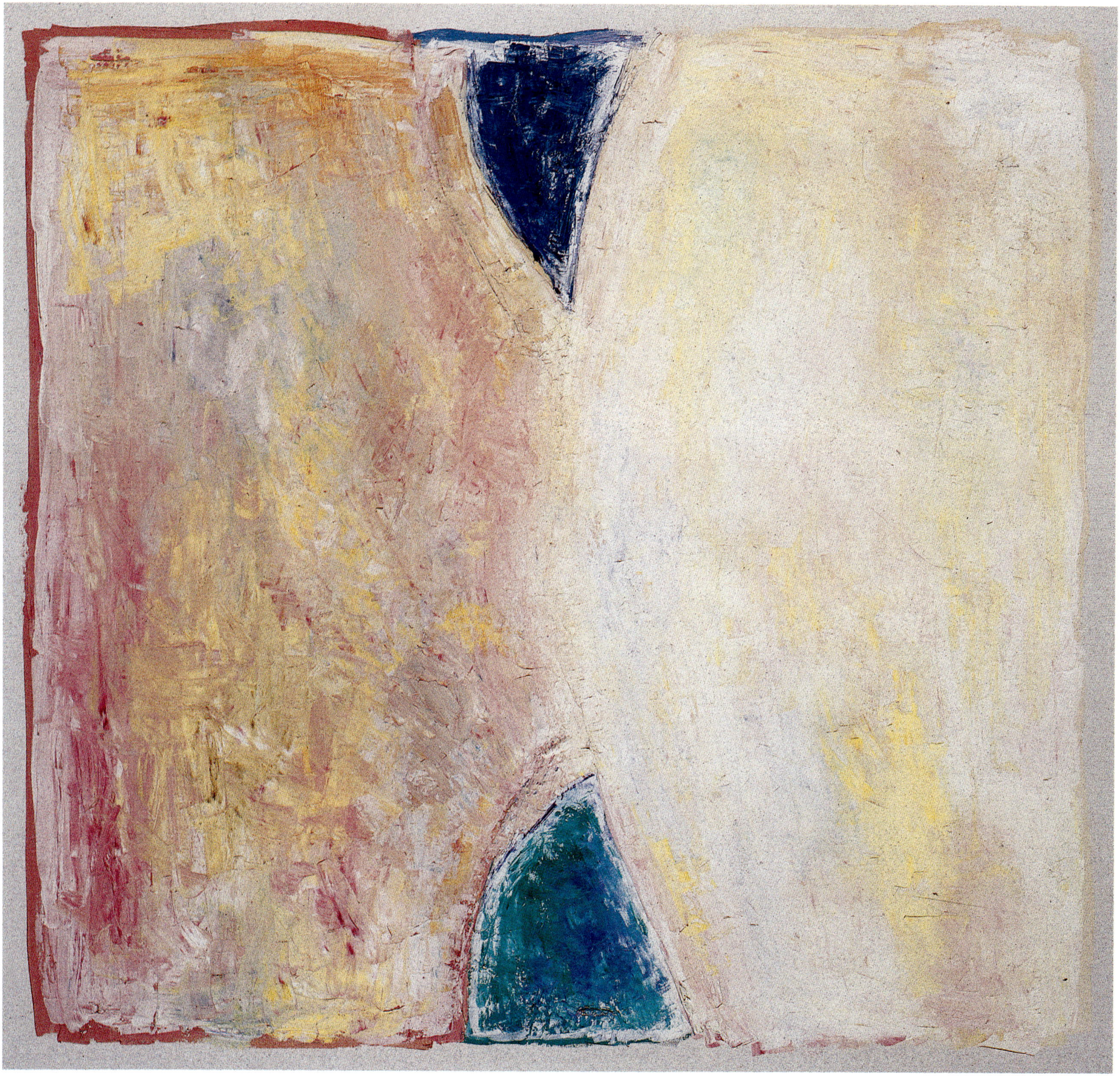

27

Madly did I kiss

The wooing arms which held me…

Book I 653-654

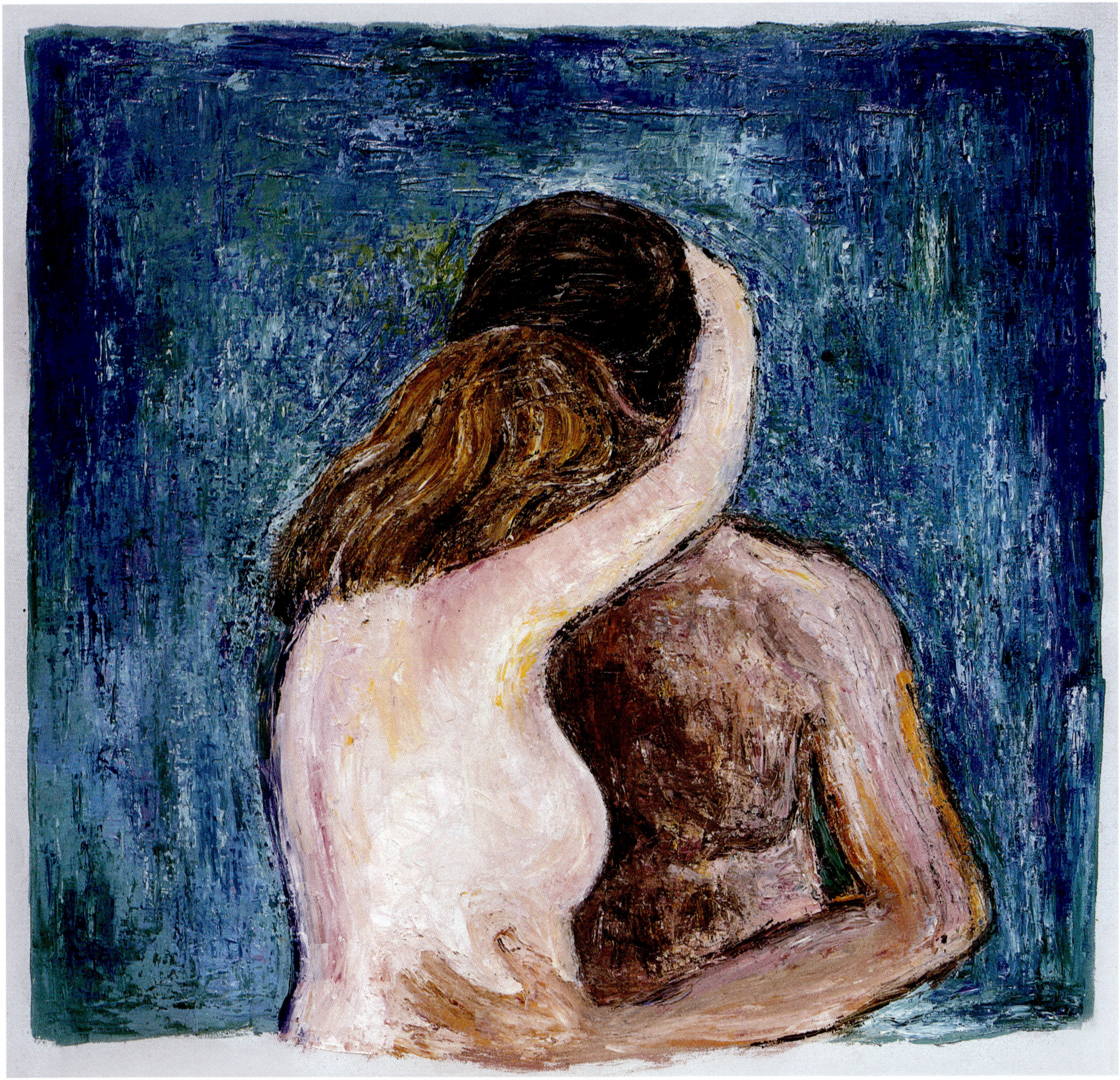

28

…I feel immortal! O my love,
My breath of life…

Book II 686-687

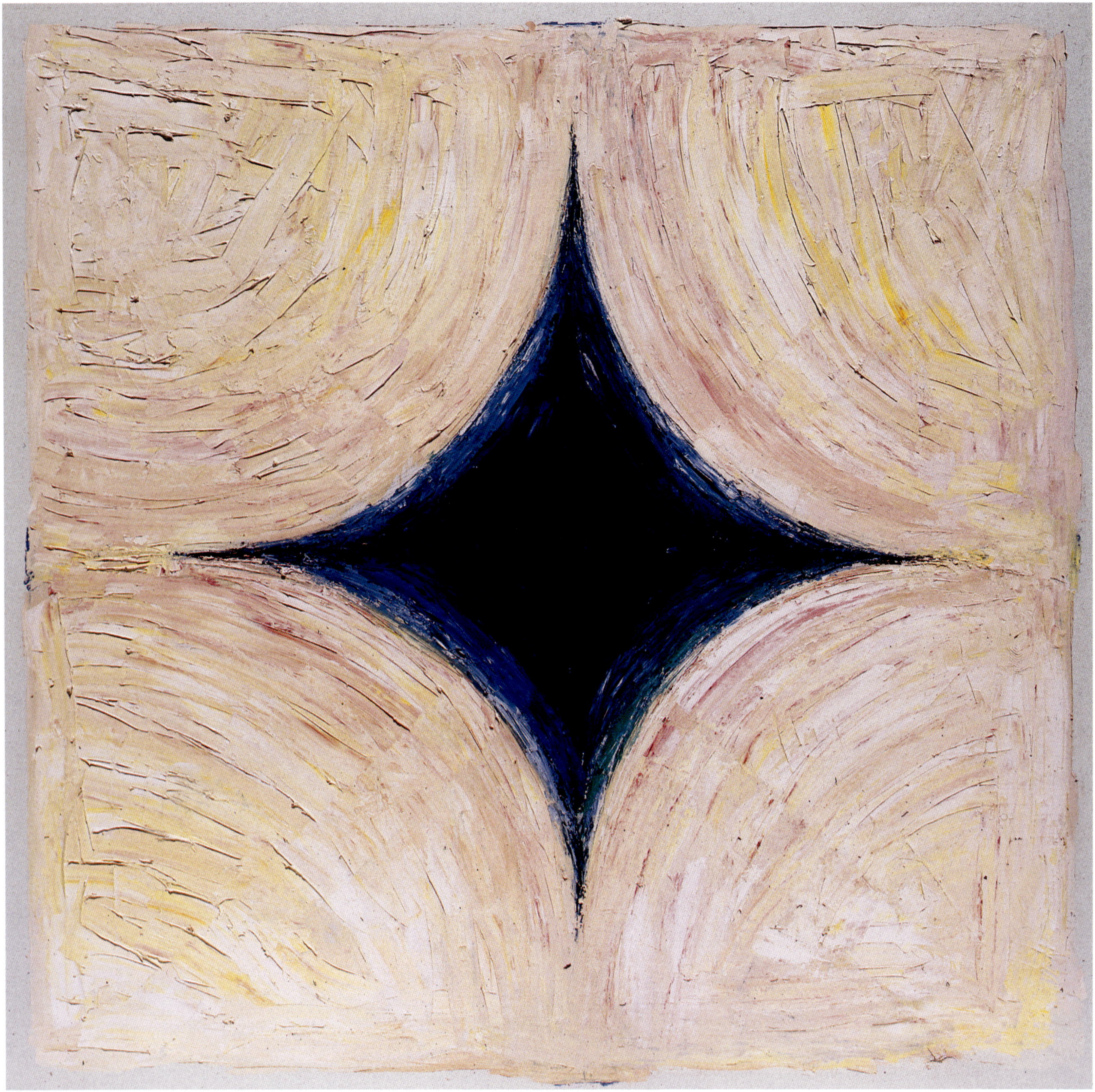

29

O dearth

Of human words! roughness of mortal speech!

Lispings empyrean will I sometime teach

Thine honied tongue–lute-breathings, which I gasp

To have thee understand, now while I clasp

Thee thus, and weep for fondness–

Book II 817-822

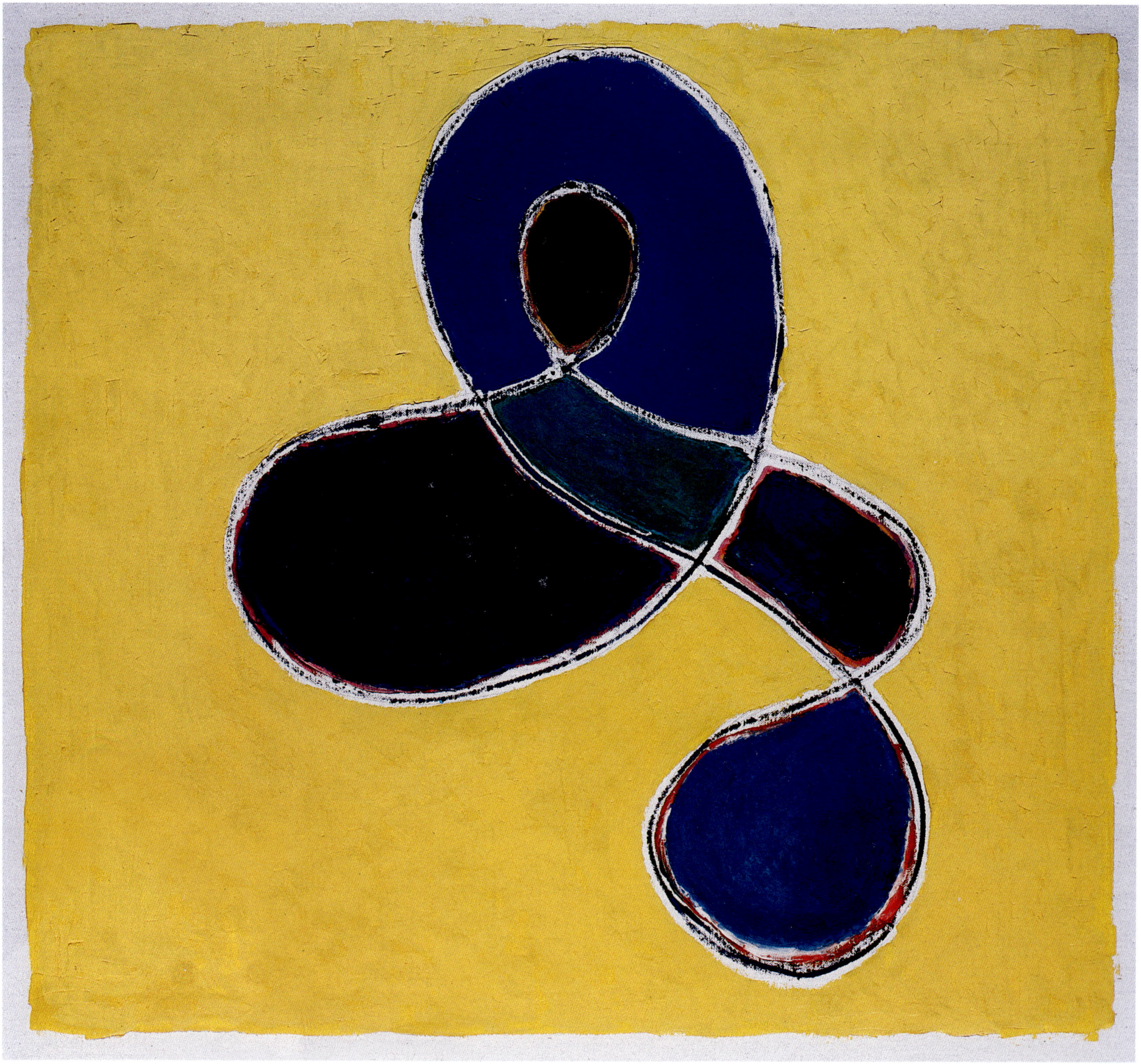

30

Ere long I will exalt thee to the shine
Of heaven ambroisal; and we will shade
Ourselves whole summers by a river glade;
And I will tell thee stories of the sky,
And breathe thee whispers of its minstrelsy.
My happy love will overwing all bounds!

Book II 809-814

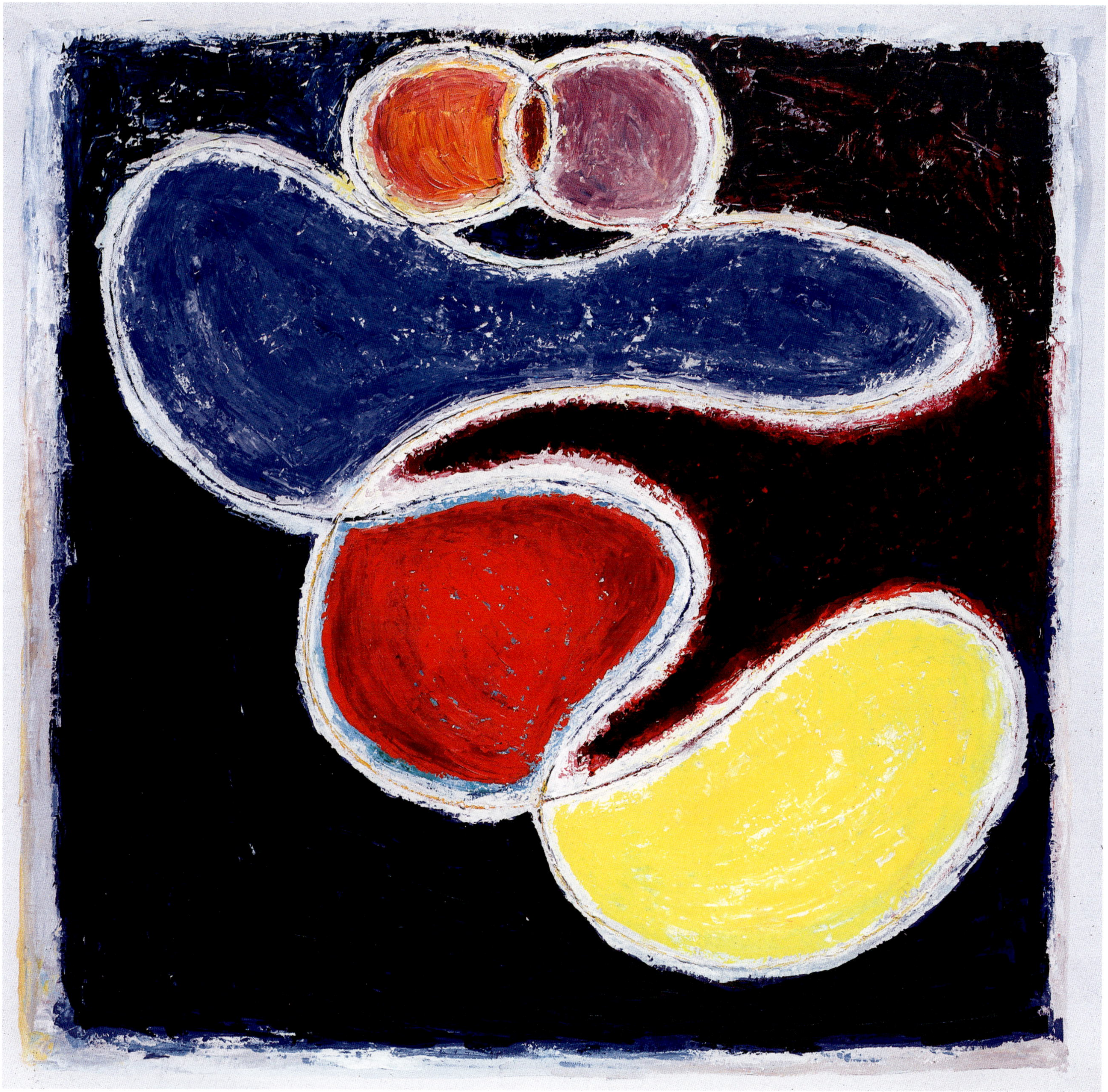

31

O thou wouldst joy to live in such a place;
Dusk for our loves, yet light enough to grace
Those gentle limbs on mossy bed reclined:
For by one step the blue sky shouldst thou find,
And by another, in deep dell below,
See, through the trees, a little river go
All in its mid-day gold and glimmering.

Book IV 675-681

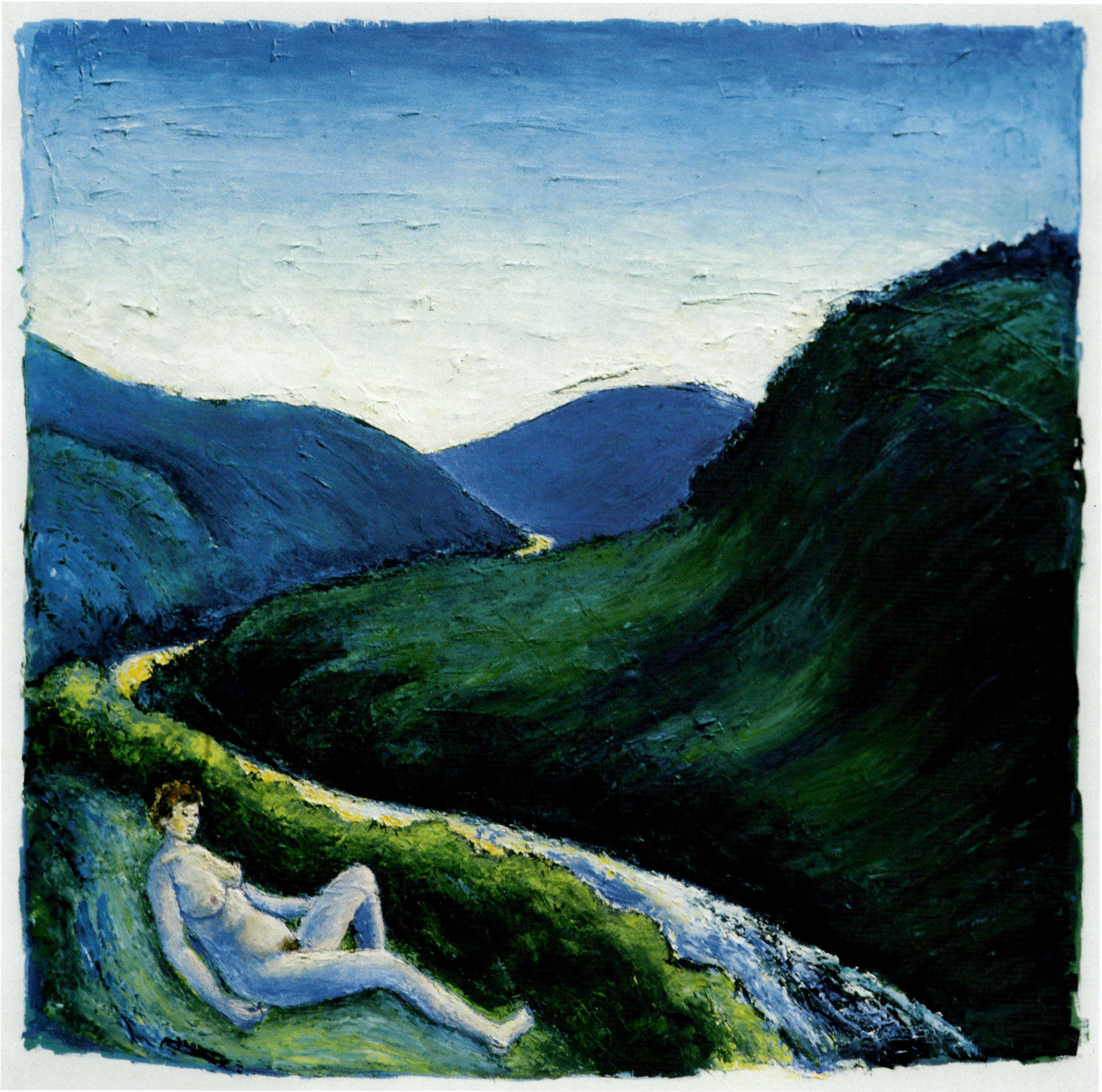

32

If thou art ripe to taste a long love dream;
If smiles, if dimples, tongues for ardour mute,
Hang in thy vision like a tempting fruit,
O let me pluck it for thee.

Book III 440-443

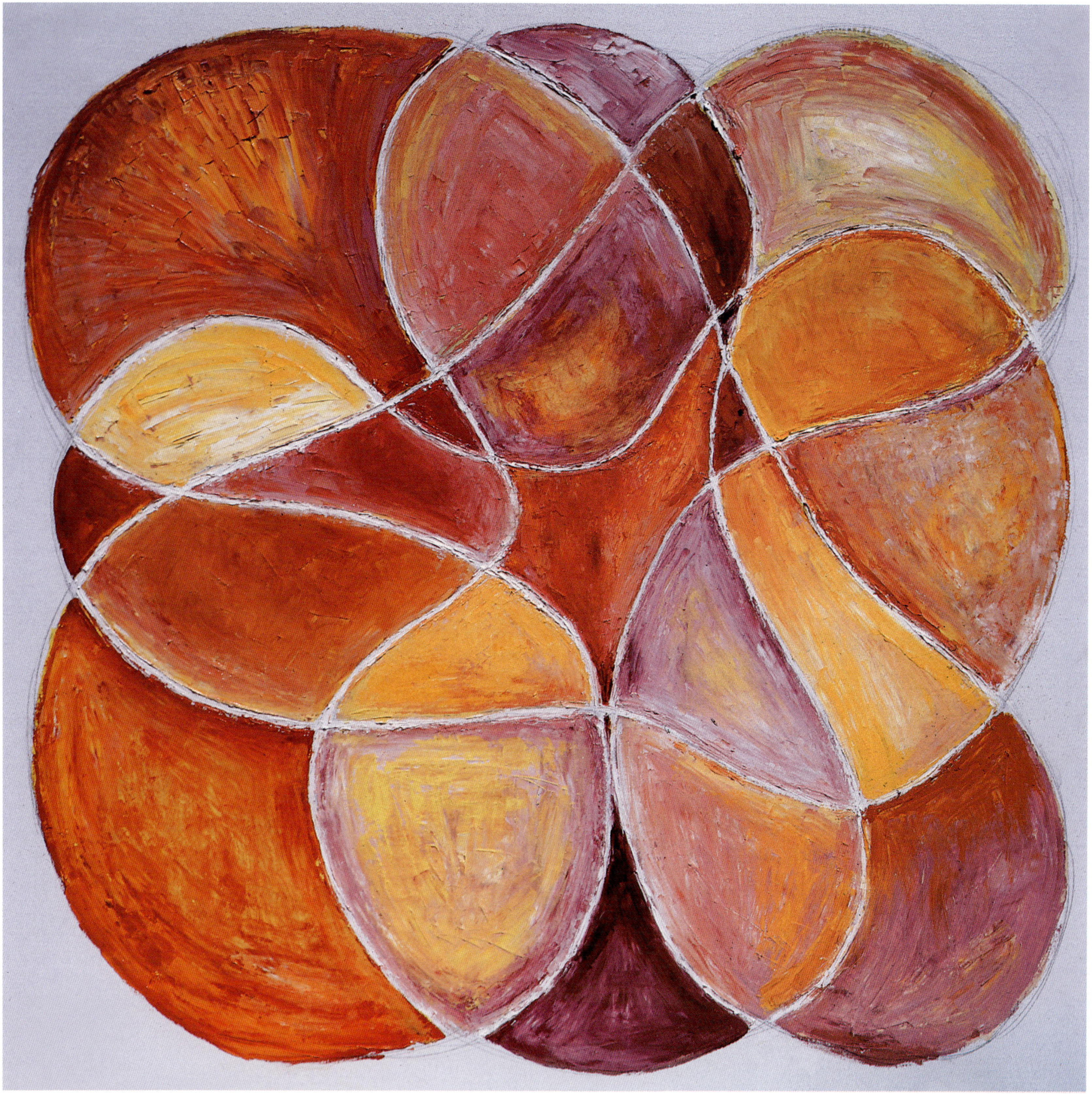

33

Now a soft kiss–
Aye, by that kiss, I vow an endless bliss,
An immortality of passion's thine...

Book II 806-808

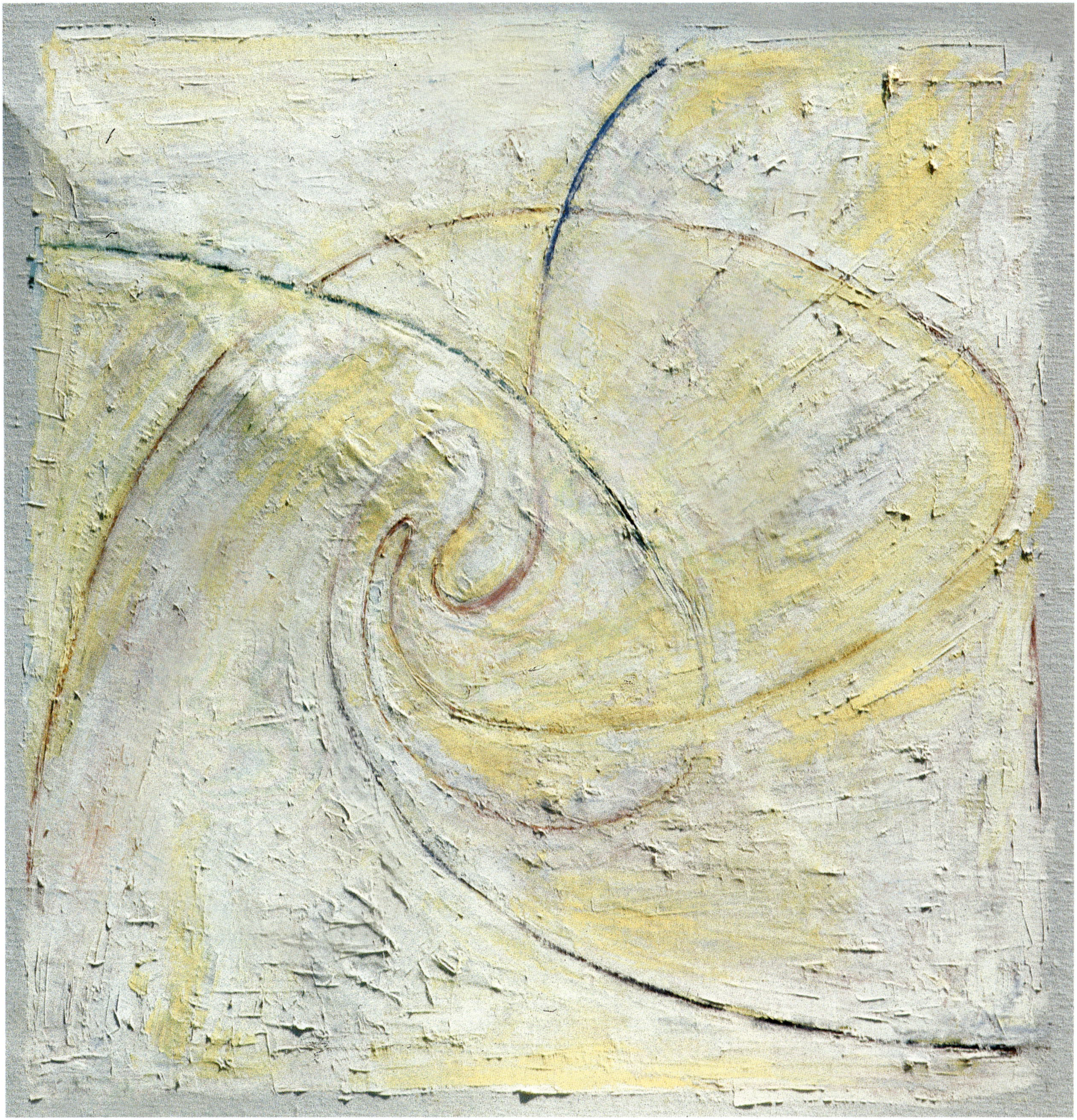

34

I do think the bars
That kept my spirit in are burst – that I
Am sailing with thee through the dizzy sky!

Book II 185-187

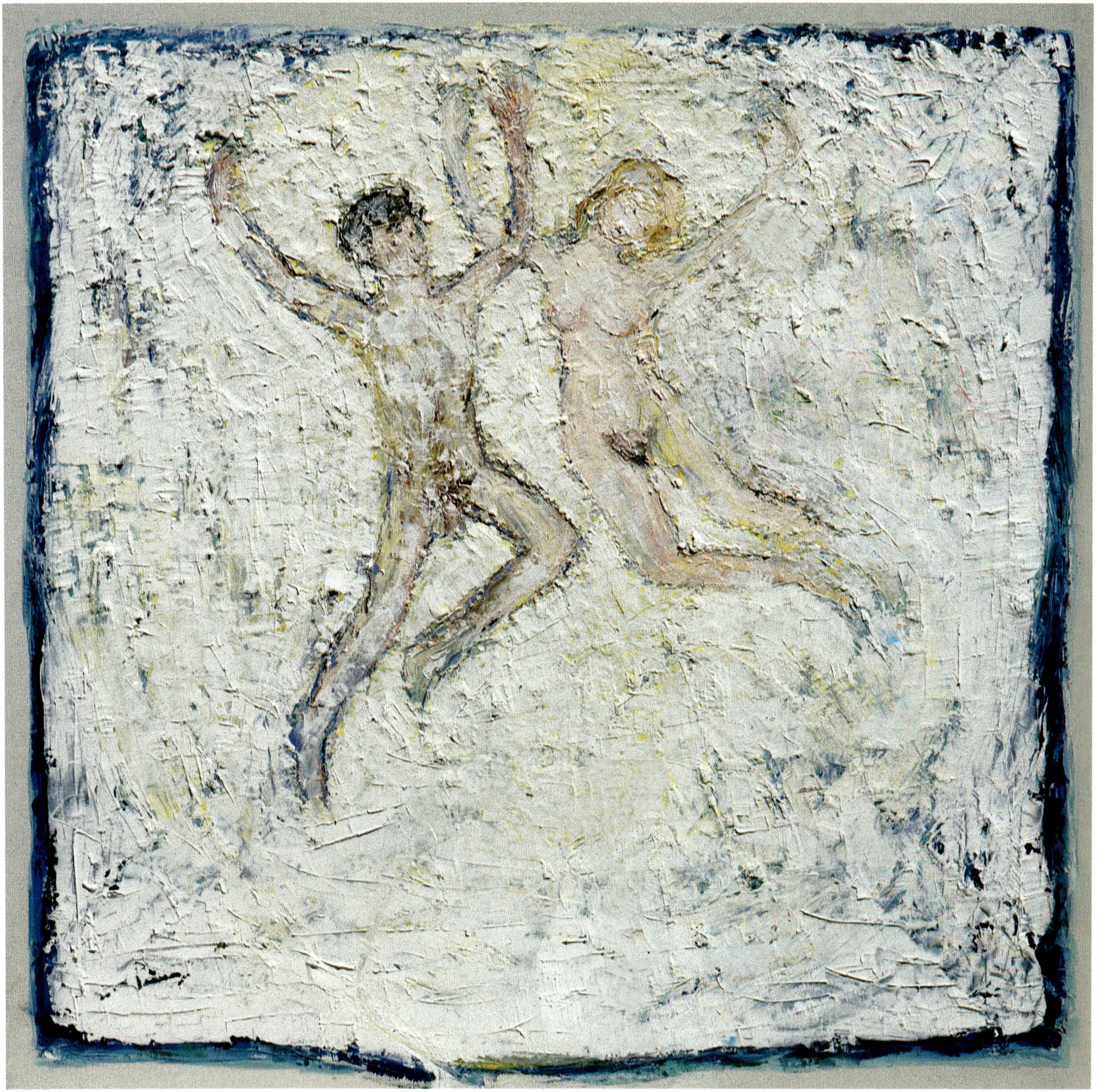

35

...this earthly love has power to make
Men's being mortal, immortal...

Book I 843-844

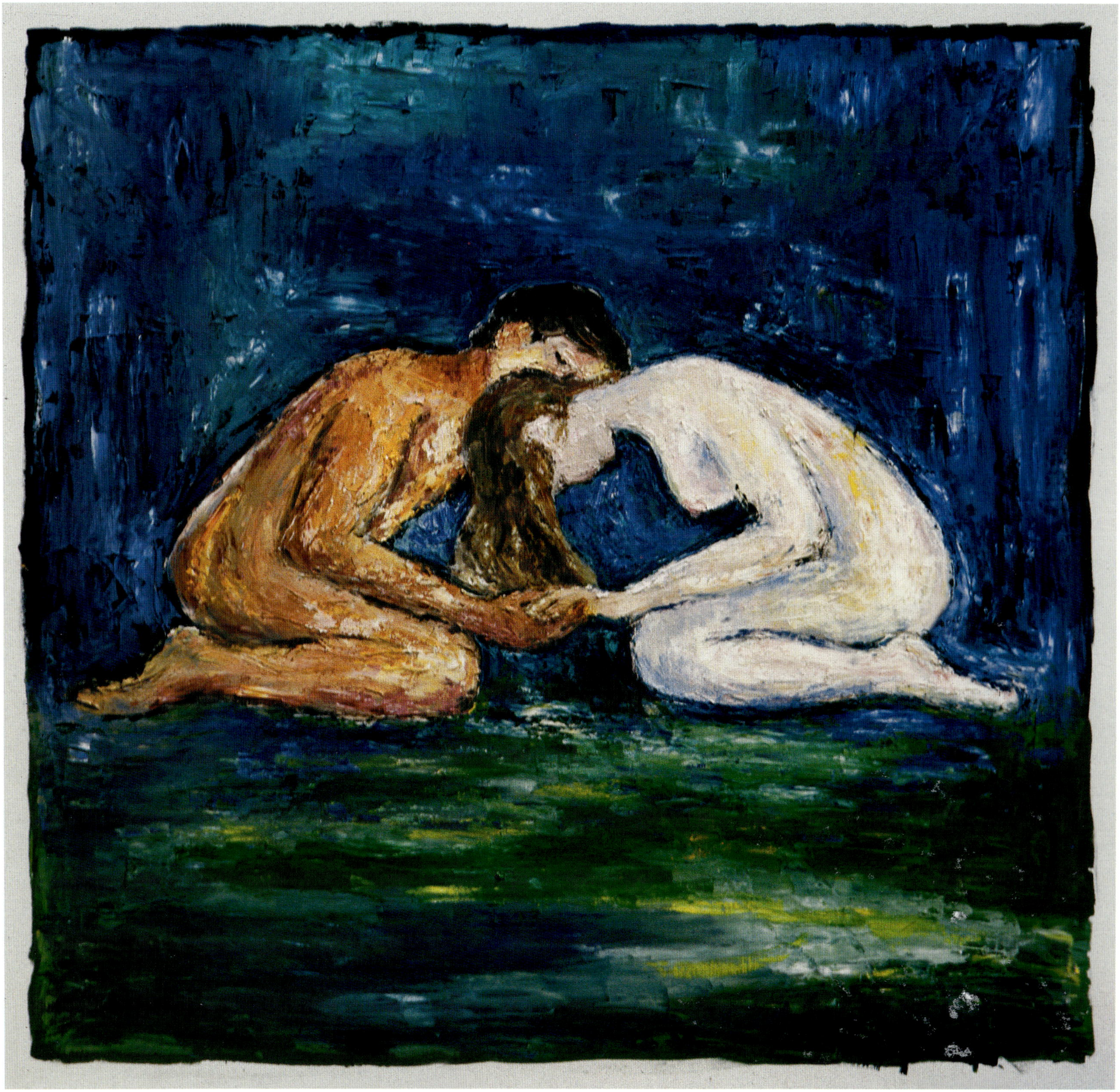

36

O let me melt into thee; let the sounds
Of our close voices marry at their birth;
Let us entwine hoveringly…

Book II 815-817

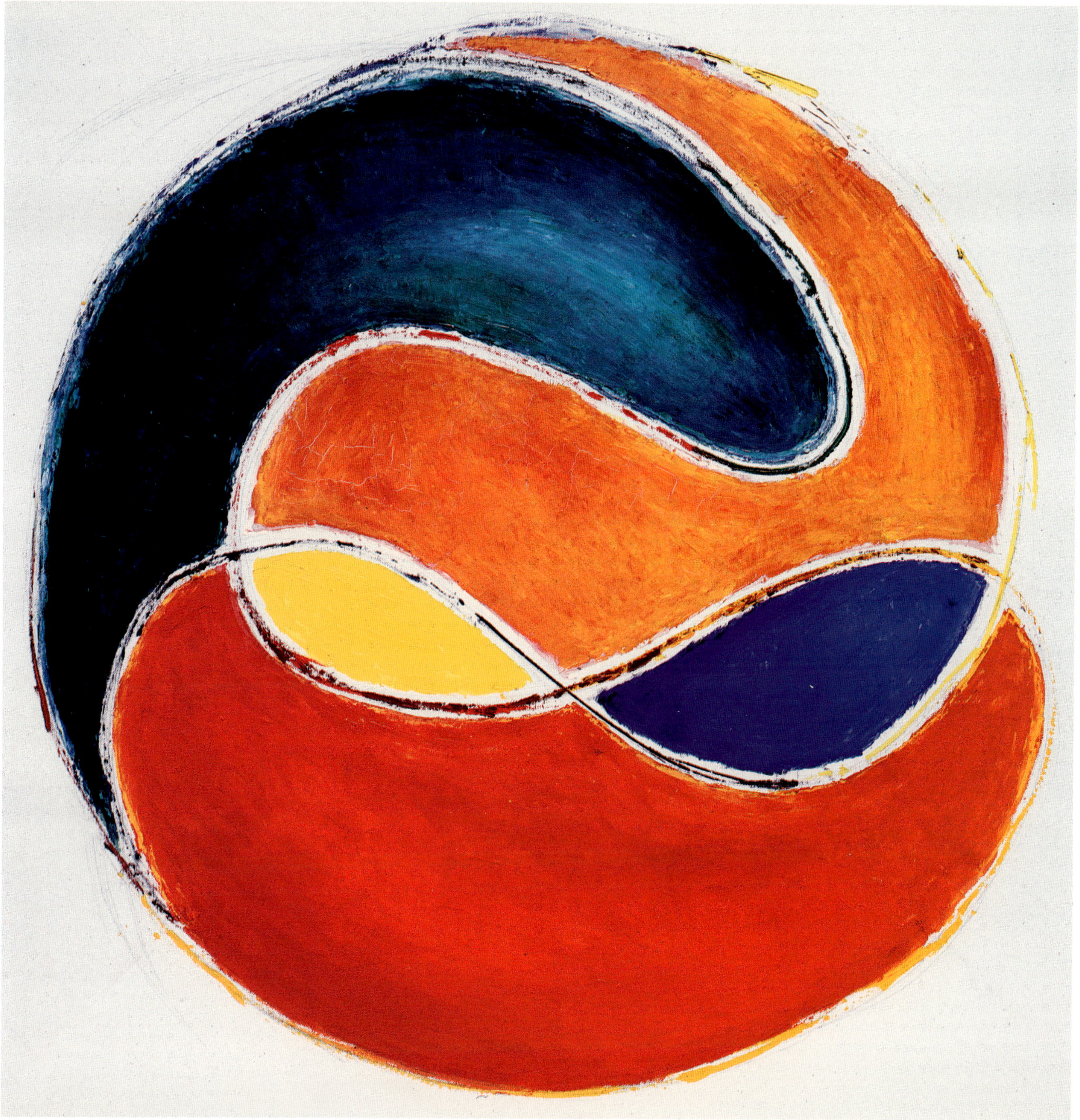

37

...that moment have we stepped
Into a sort of oneness, and our state
Is like a floating spirit's...

Book I 795-797

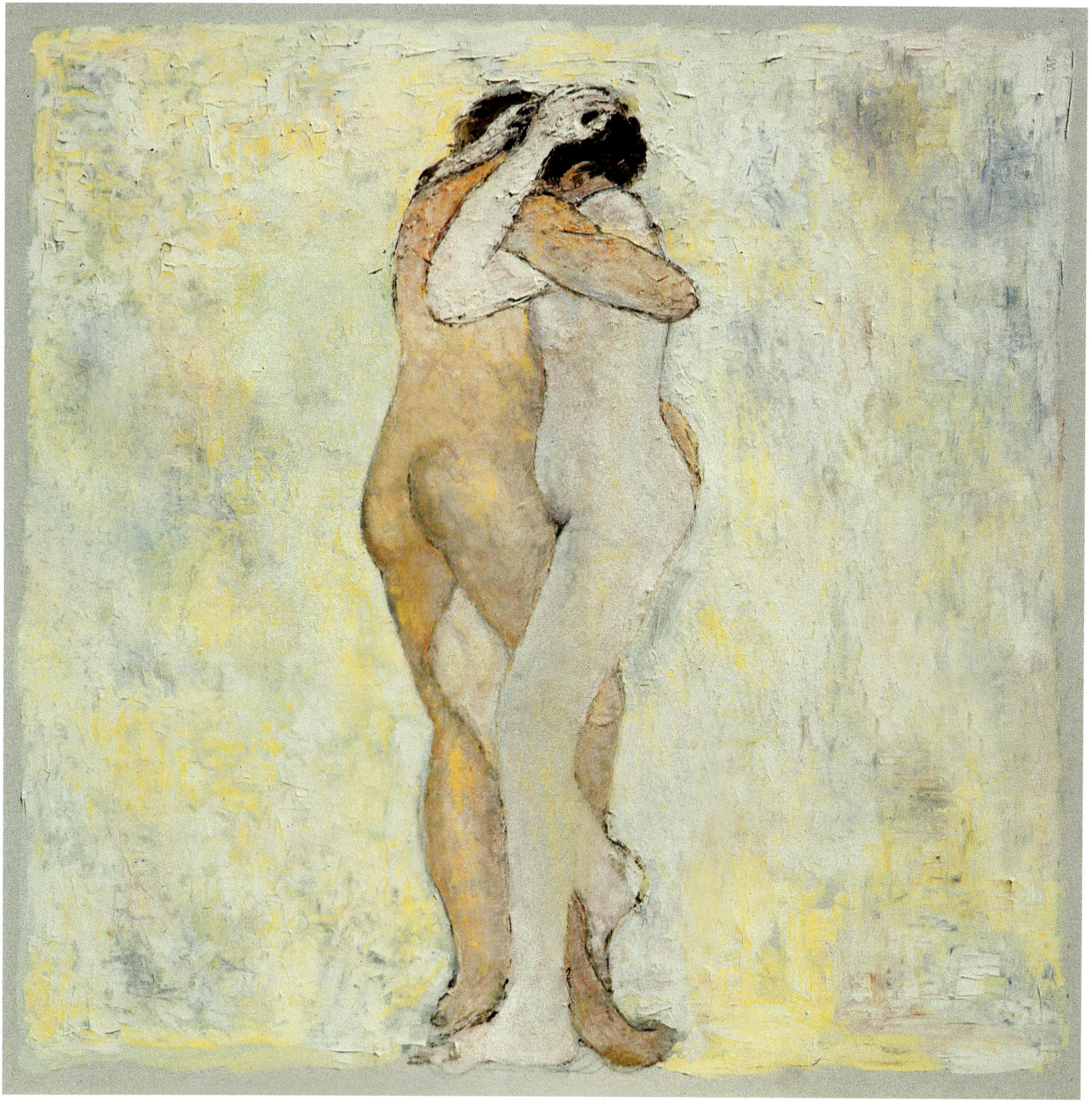

38

O known unknown! from whom my being sips
Such darling essence, wherefore may I not
Be ever in these arms?

Book II 739-741

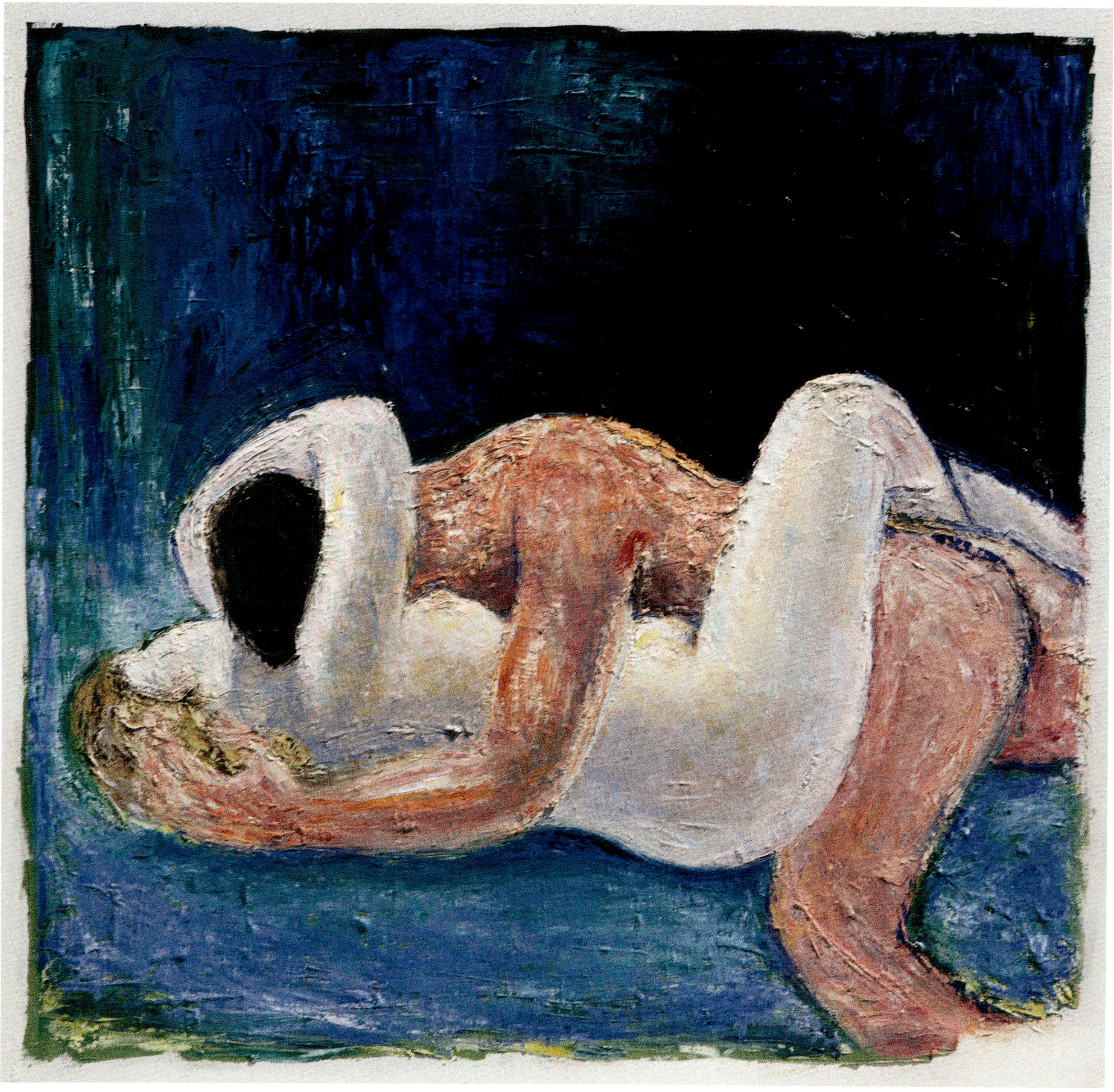

39

Be still a symbol of immensity;
A firmament reflected in a sea…

Book I 299-300

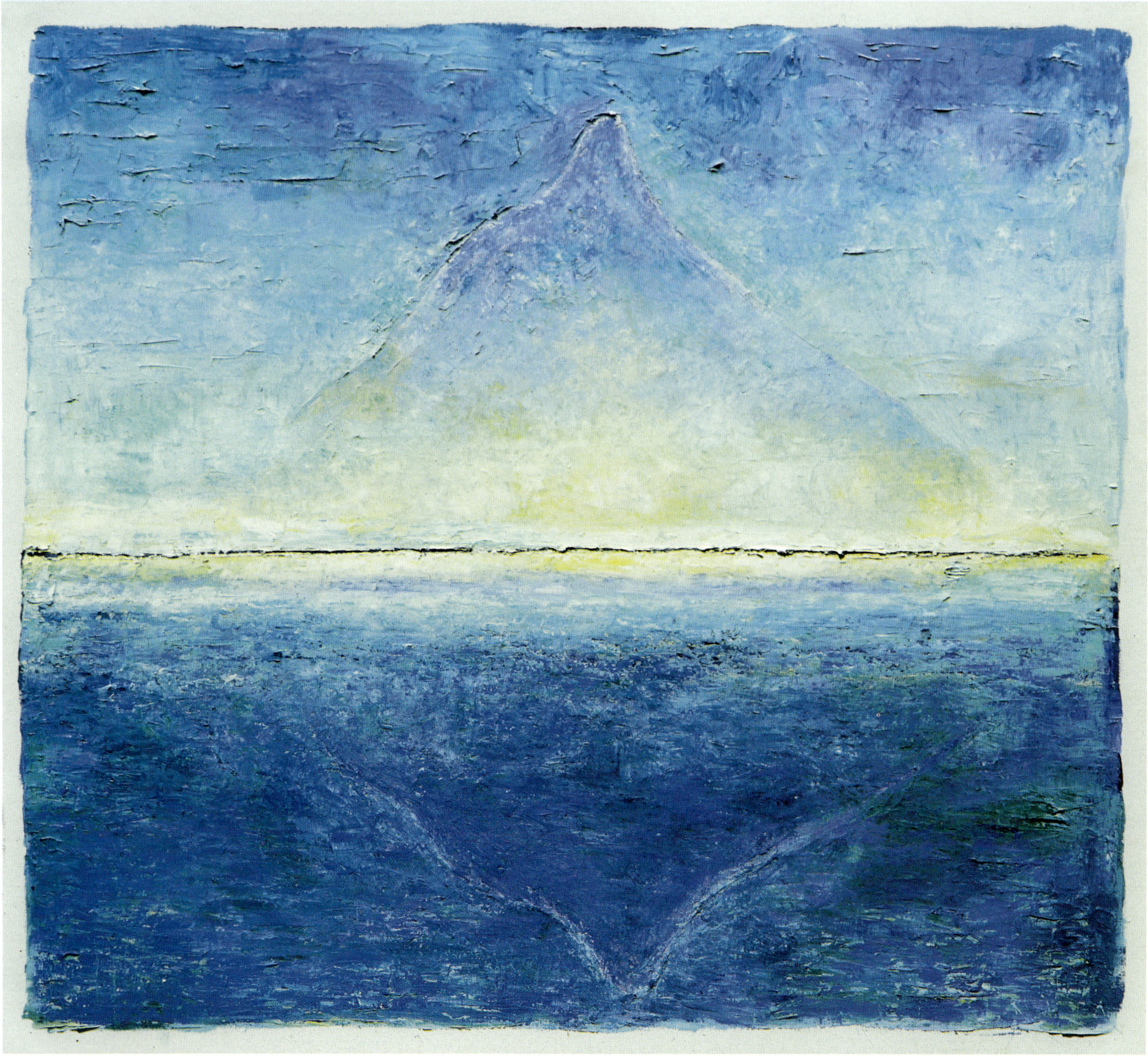

40

We might die;

We might embrace and die: voluptuous thought!

Book IV 758-759

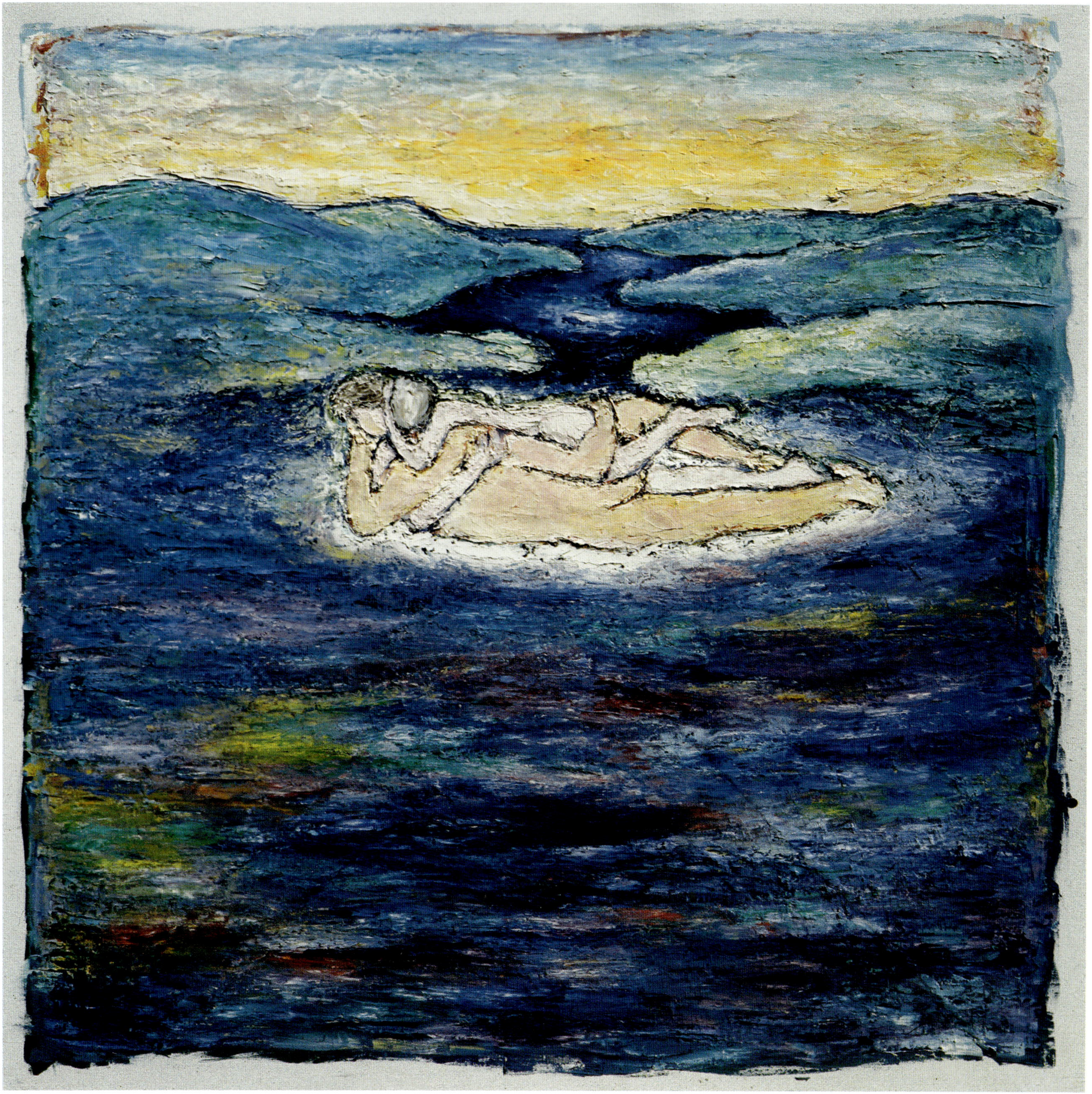

41

O did he ever live, that lonely man,
Who lov'd – and music slew not? 'Tis the pest
Of love, that fairest joys give most unrest;
That things of delicate and tenderest worth
Are swallow'd all, and made a seared dearth,
By one consuming flame: it doth immerse
And suffocate true blessings in a curse.

Book II 364-370

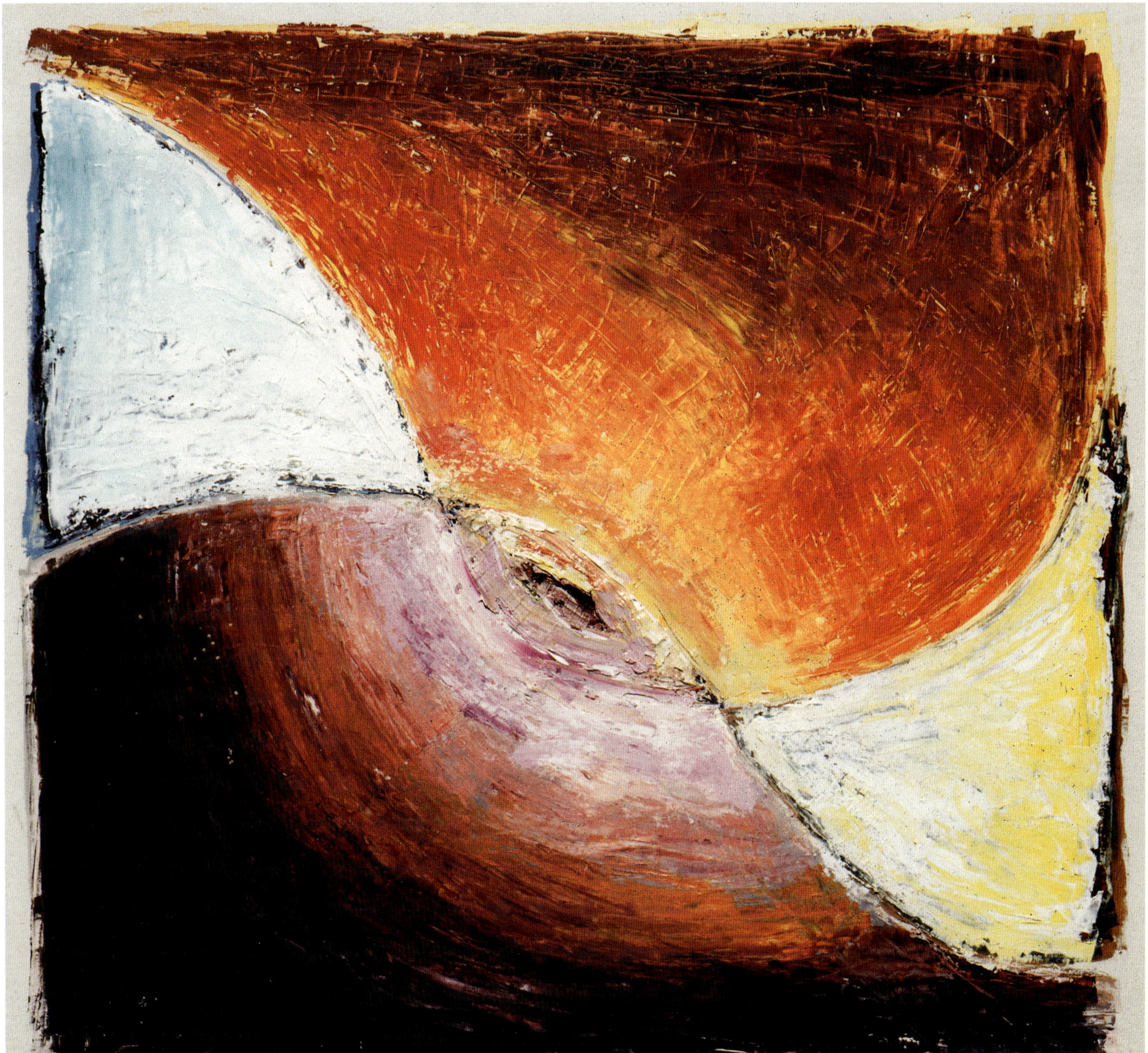

42

Apollo's upward fire
Made every eastern cloud a silvery pyre…

Book I 95-96

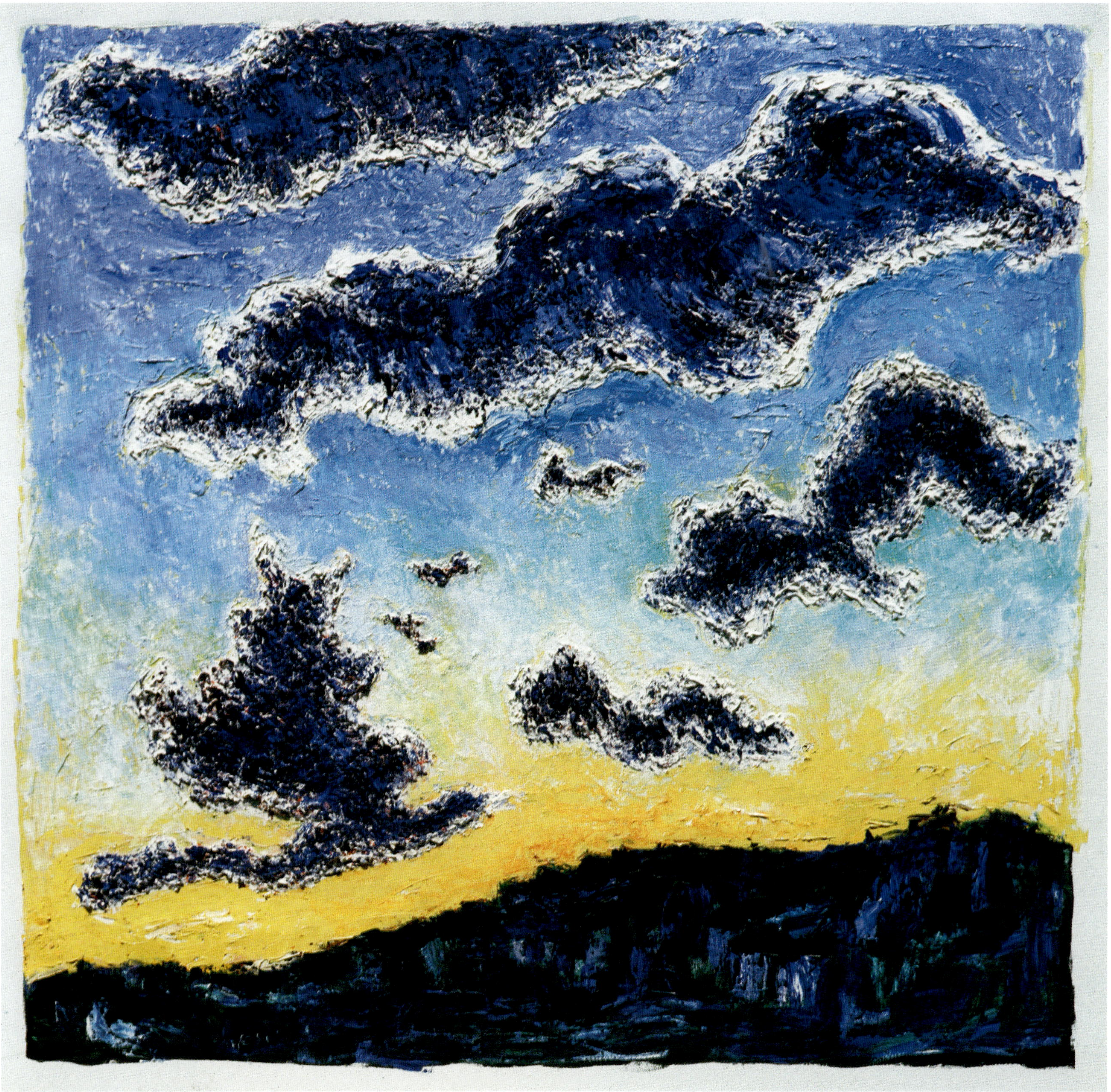

43

An endless fountain of immortal drink,
Pouring unto us from the heaven's brink.

Book I 23-24

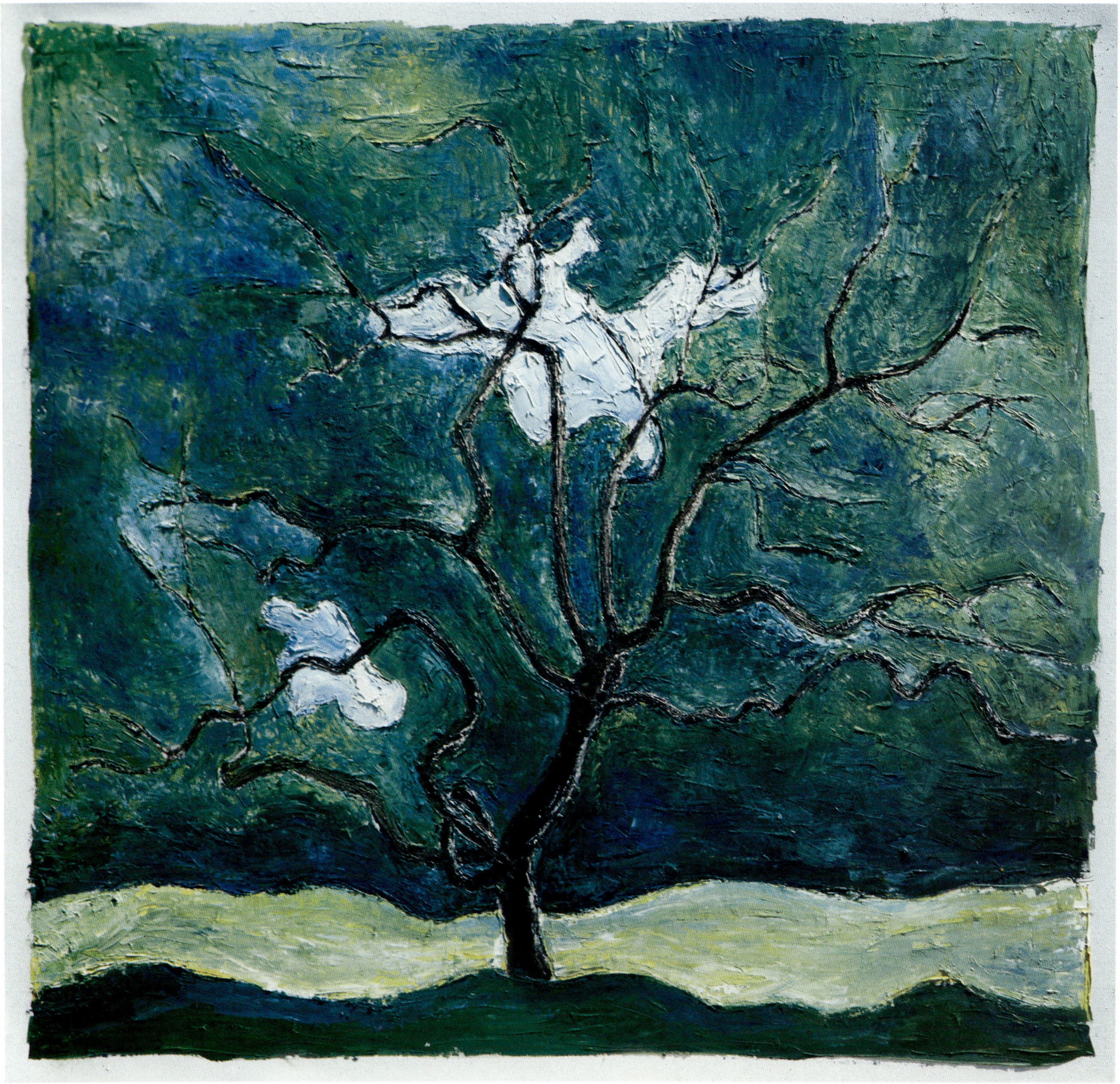

44

He ne'er is crown'd
With immortality, who fears to follow
Where airy voices lead...

Book II 211-213

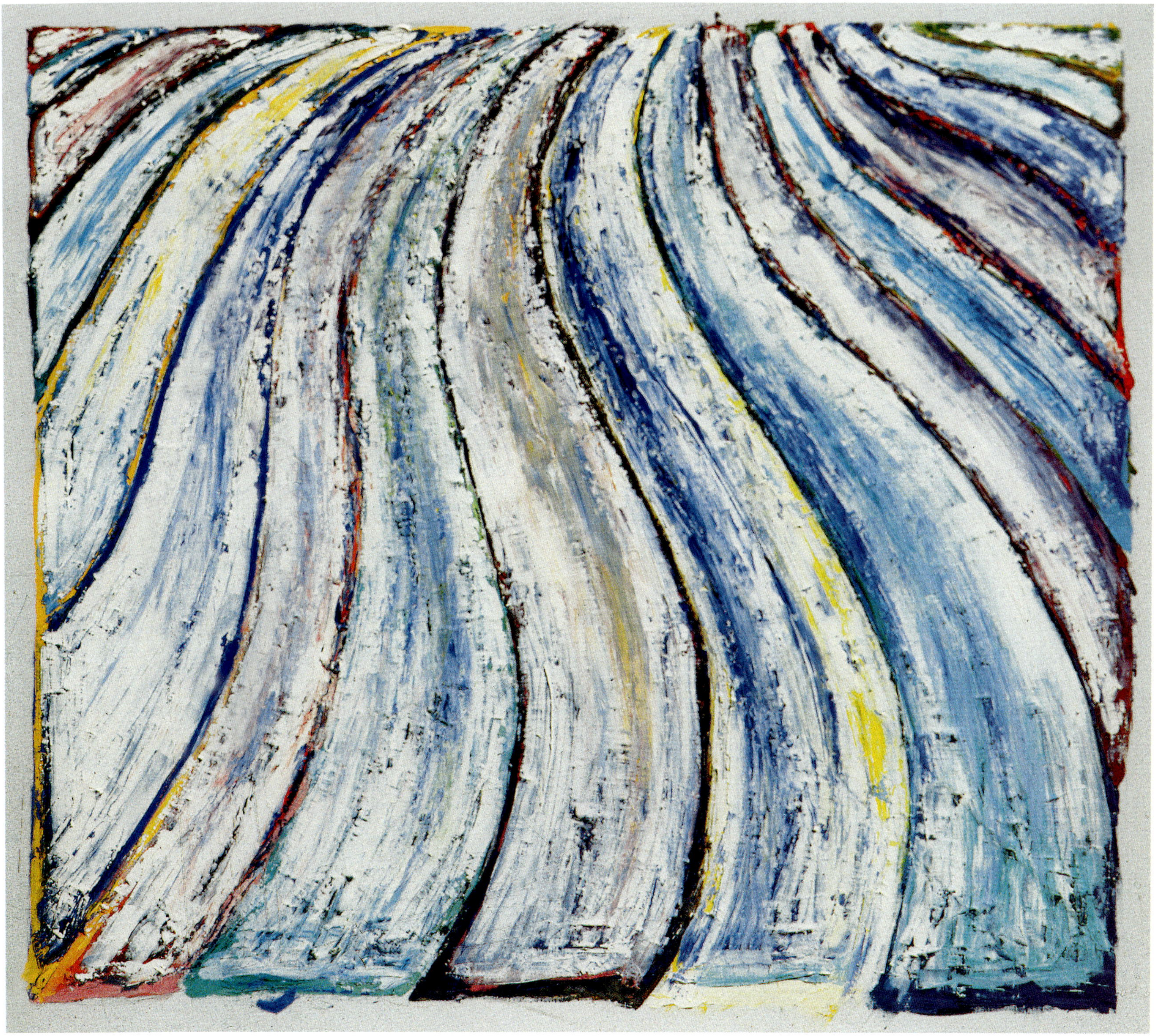